The Lion of God
Archangel Ari'El

...Personal Encounters

Carol P. Vaccariello, D.Min., LPC

BALBOA.
PRESS
A DIVISION OF HAY HOUSE

Copyright © 2017 Carol P. Vaccariello, D.Min., LPC.

All rights reserved. No part of this book may be used or reproduced by any means, graphic, electronic, or mechanical, including photocopying, recording, taping or by any information storage retrieval system without the written permission of the author except in the case of brief quotations embodied in critical articles and reviews.

Balboa Press books may be ordered through booksellers or by contacting:

Balboa Press
A Division of Hay House
1663 Liberty Drive
Bloomington, IN 47403
www.balboapress.com
1 (877) 407-4847

Because of the dynamic nature of the Internet, any web addresses or links contained in this book may have changed since publication and may no longer be valid. The views expressed in this work are solely those of the author and do not necessarily reflect the views of the publisher, and the publisher hereby disclaims any responsibility for them.

The author of this book does not dispense medical advice or prescribe the use of any technique as a form of treatment for physical, emotional, or medical problems without the advice of a physician, either directly or indirectly. The intent of the author is only to offer information of a general nature to help you in your quest for emotional and spiritual well-being. In the event you use any of the information in this book for yourself, which is your constitutional right, the author and the publisher assume no responsibility for your actions.

Any people depicted in stock imagery provided by Thinkstock are models, and such images are being used for illustrative purposes only.
Certain stock imagery © Thinkstock.

Print information available on the last page.

ISBN: 978-1-5043-7519-1 (sc)
ISBN: 978-1-5043-7521-4 (hc)
ISBN: 978-1-5043-7520-7 (e)

Library of Congress Control Number: 2017902446

Balboa Press rev. date: 02/18/2017

CONTENTS

ACKNOWLEDGMENTS

First, I am grateful to Grandfather and Great Mother, for inviting me into this sacred, abundant journey.

I am grateful to:

My faithful, eternal companion and guide in this adventure, Archangel Ari'El, for protecting me, loving me, guiding me, and impressing upon me the importance of publishing these stories.

Those who have gone before me, the Ancestors, on whose shoulders I stand: Mom, Dad, Frank, Richard and many more who join with me daily in prayer.

Visionary mentor, colleague and friend, the Reverend Doctor Matthew Fox, for challenging me, modeling the critical importance of engaging my inner guides, creativity and mysticism.

"Nephew" and confidant, F. Christopher Reynolds, for showing up, daily kitchen table conversations, creating the kitchen wall storyboard, deep knowing and confidence, seeing in me more than I do.

Niece and daughter-in-spirit, Jessie Pritchard, for being the first to read the chapters allowing me to see the wonder in her eyes and hear her words of excitement, for helping me believe these stories are compelling and need to be shared by someone like me.

Friend and secretary, Vicki Grace, for a warm and cheery disposition that I can count on, for technical skill creating this book's cover and making me look good.

Adopted son, Michael Olin-Hitt, for sharing your writing skills and constructive criticism. You have infused light and clarity to these chapters.

Professor, Dean and mentor, the Reverend Doctor John Biersdorf, who challenged me to open my heart and soul to new ways of knowing through dreams and visions.

FOREWORD

Reading this surprising book with its surprising ending reminds me of two encounters in my life. The first was with the widow of David Paladin, the Navajo painter who was initiated as a shaman through a particularly painful episode as a young soldier. Lying about his age at sixteen to get into the army in the Second World War, he was sent to Europe to fight and was almost immediately captured. He was imprisoned not in a GI camp but in a concentration camp where he was the only Native American among the other inmates and was tortured periodically. For example, one Christmas one foot was nailed to the floor and he was ordered to twirl on that foot for twenty-four hours. When after four years the Americans liberated that camp they found David's comatose body—which weighed all of 65 pounds—at the bottom of a pile of dead bodies. He was returned to his reservation in Arizona and after two years, on coming out of his coma, his elders said to him: "You have a choice. You are a paraplegic so you can go into a veteran's hospital where you will live in a wheelchair the rest of your life. Or: We can try to heal you in the ancient way."

He chose to be healed in the ancient way so they took him to an ice-cold river and threw him in over his head. He said when he hit the water he was more angry at his elders than at the Nazis who tortured him. But it worked. He got his legs back and made two pilgrimages to Mexico and back on foot. Being an artist, he also met Marc Chagall and Picasso as a young man and Chagall said to him: "Don't paint the stories of your people; paint your dreams of the stories of your people." This, he testified, gave him his freedom to be his own kind of artist.

I learned about David through his wife who invited me to contribute to an exhibit of his work after he died since, as it turned out, he had read my books such as *Original Blessing* and appreciated how my theology helped reconcile his Native American and Christian spiritual traditions. Later I visited his widow Lynda Paladin in the home where they had lived and he had painted over the years and she told me this story. "Often," she said, "dead painters would come and visit my husband during the night and ask him to paint a picture which he did and it was their picture, not his." Then she left the room and came back with a picture and as soon as I saw it I said, "That's by Paul Klee." And sure enough it was signed "Paul Klee" at the bottom. "I remember the night that Paul Klee came to visit him and dictated this picture," she said.

I share this story to remind the reader that life is more interesting and boasts far more dimensions than our culture dares to tell us. We live in many worlds at once. David Paladin's elders told him late in his life that the reason he suffered so much as a young man was to initiate him as a shaman.[1] Shamans are often people who went through deep struggle in their youth—a shattering experience that often has the effect of shattering the psyche with the result that they live in more than one world at once.

The stories that Carol Vaccariello shares in this moving book are of this kind as well. Her visitations with angels are special but also very real and they bear close attention. "By their fruits you will know them," says Jesus. Carol, whom I have known for over twenty years, is very real, very grounded, very hard working; she is a keen, serious listener and teacher, a seasoned student and administrator. She is committed to service and lives a simple life style of service to others. She has lived and worked as a Catholic sister for five years; as a wife and supporter of a union organizer in Ohio for thirty years; as a Protestant pastor for thirty-one years; and as co-director of the Doctor of Ministry program at my school the University of Creation Spirituality for nine years; and later at Wisdom University; she has served as an interim pastor at a number of UCC churches, often called in to resolve conflicts or to help heal wounded congregations. Her feet are very much on the ground. The fruits of her healthy and giving life are there for anyone to see. The stories in this book reveal another and more hidden side to Carol yet they are stories we can all heed and learn from. It is courageous of her to share them.

A second encounter that comes to mind on reading this book is my friendship with Lorna Byrne. Lorna, who was born and grew up in the west coast of Ireland and was dyslexic and was never taught to read and write, is today a mother and grandmother. She has been in

---

[1] For David's story and painting see *Painting the Dream: The Visionary Art of Navojo Painter David Chethlahe Paladin* (Rochester, Vt: Park Street Press, 1992.

communication with angels since she was two years old. They told her not to tell anyone until they gave her the word—which was not until her husband died some eight years ago or so. Since then she has dictated several books on her encounters with the angels that have become international best sellers. They include *Angels in My Hair; Stairways to Heaven* and *A Message of Hope from the Angels.*

I had the privilege of meeting Lorna first in New York City and then by interviewing her at Grace Cathedral in San Francisco before about 1300 people. (The night before we celebrated a Cosmic Mass with the theme of the Angels in Silicon Valley at the Institute of Transpersonal Psychology, and I interviewed her briefly during the Mass. She reported to me afterwards that there were lots of angels there, "far more angels than people," she said.) In our interview at Grace Cathedral she said this: "There are lots of unemployed angels in the world today." I said: "Oh, no! I know so many unemployed people—are you telling me we have to put all kind of angels to work as well?" To this she replied: "This is the situation. God knows how much trouble people are in today and is pouring angels onto the earth to help humans, but no one is asking them for help. Thus, many unemployed angels."

This exchange reminds me very much of the message in Carol's book. We humans clearly have the capacity to interact with spirits or angels, beings different from ourselves, and we need to at this critical time in history. Frequently I have asked audiences I speak to to shut their eyes and then raise their hands if they have had encounters with angels or someone they trust has had such encounters. Usually about 80% of the audience raises their hands.

We need the help of the spirits or angels today not only because otherwise angels eager to help us are unemployed but especially because as a species we are doing badly and it is clear we need all the help we can get. In my book *The Physics of Angels* that I wrote with scientist Rupert Sheldrake, we dialogued on the topic of angels. Among many lessons I learned was the teaching of Thomas Aquinas that angels "cannot help but love" and that angels "learn exclusively from intuition."[2] This is very telling because intuition, as Albert Einstein has pointed out, is what is missing in our society these days. The academic system is rigged to serve the left brain, the analytic brain, almost exclusively. It is far easier to measure quantitative and verbal realities emanating from the left brain than the truths—including values—that emanate from the right hemisphere of the brain where intuition and feeling and mysticism are birthed. Einstein warns us that values do not come from the rational brain but from the intuitive brain. Here is what Einstein says: "The intuitive mind is a sacred gift and our rational mind is a faithful servant. We have created a society that honors the servant and has forgotten the gift."

A book like this breaks through the censoring of our right brain and its rich experiences. It opens the door to our often-closed intuitive brain. Some at first glance will find it hard to face, but that is because of the bias of our culture and the one-sided education so characteristic of our culture. Other cultures, indigenous and pre-modern, have not been so narrow or so shut down to their intuitive brain. This is why Carol has been asked by those from the angelic realm to speak out and tell her story: Because humans need this for survival. As Einstein teaches, values do not come from our rational brains but from our intuitive brains. Thus, from the kind of opening

---

[2] See Matthw Fox and Rupert Sheldrake, *The Physics of Angels: Exploring the Realm Where Science and Spirit Meet* (Rhinebeck, NY: Monkfish Book Publishing 2014)

up and humble receptivity that Carol embodies in this book. Do our values need awakening? Deepening? Expanding at this time of human and planetary history? Of course they do.

Ours is a time for people who have encountered spirits and angels to come out of the closet. The modern age is over. We live in a post-modern age with deep needs such as reinventing politics, education, economics, religion and the media. Time is running out for our species. We can be grateful that Carol Vaccariello has had the courage to step up and share her angelic experiences with us. This invites others to follow.

Therefore we can all be thankful for this book and we should muster the courage that Carol has mustered to share her experiences with us to actually read the book, turn it over in our hearts and minds, and ask what the angels and spirits are asking of us. Thank you, Carol, for your straight-forward telling of special events. If we pay attention we will all be the better for it. And Mother Earth will heal and be better off, too, when humans get their values shaken up and rearranged. Thank you, angels and spirits for your visits to this grounded and humble (meaning humus or earth-connected) woman who is sharing your messages in this book.

The Reverend Doctor Matthew Fox is one of the spiritual giants of our time. Dr. Fox has invested his life developing and teaching the tradition of Creation Spirituality authoring thirty-three books. (www.matthewfox.org)

INTRODUCTION

I walk with Beauty before me,
I walk with Beauty behind me.
I walk with Beauty above me,
I walk with Beauty below me,
I walk with Beauty beside me,
I walk with Beauty all around me,
I walk with Beauty inside me.
Navaho Beauty Chant

Often when I lead prayer, I teach this Beauty-filled Navaho Chant. Beauty is one way to speak about *God:* the All-in-One and the One-in-All.

When I was a child, I was taught that prayer was lifting our minds and hearts to God. As soon as I brought my awareness to prayer, I would sense the Sacred Presence. I continue to pray in that way. I am aware of the Sacred, the Spirit. I believe we live in a

Spirit-filled reality. Some have developed a habit of prayer that helps to create an acute awareness of the Sacred. The events that I am about to share with you don't seem odd or strange to me because I live in a sacred reality. Each of us receives the same invitation.

Here is a way to understand this: Whatever you or I see in our daily encounters with others, we don't consider out of the ordinary. Even if we haven't seen someone for a very long time, when they show up we expect to see them, experience their presence. We expect to see others every day. We expect to carry on conversations. We expect to use telephones and computers to connect with others. We don't think any of this is strange or out of the ordinary. It is simply the way it is.

The experience of Spirit is so strong for me that I no longer consider it to be outside or other than my reality. It is a continuous tape running in the background of my awareness. When I bring my awareness to the Divine Presence, Spirit manifests. This deep connection sustains me.

For me, seeing and talking to entities of the spirit world doesn't seem strange because in many ways it is simply where I live. They are a part of my daily reality.

I believe anyone who chooses can develop this same perception of reality. It simply requires openness of heart and mind and trust that all is well. Courage dominates fear and excitement banishes boredom. Living in and with Spirit is a life of awesome adventure and becoming in ways I never dreamt possible. This book is an invitation for you. Open your heart to a more complete reality. If you are already doing that, then enjoy these tellings of a sister traveler on the spirit road. Hopefully some day you will share your stories with me. I love to hear how Spirit shows up!

Spirit is always present and longs to be connected to each of us. Connecting is so simple that we miss it. Simply pray. Pray often. Think about the Sacred. Watch for Divinity in your life. The Spirit is reaching out to us in every moment in a variety of ways. We are never coerced. We are always invited.

You will notice that I use a variety of terms to identify *God*. Traditionally every religious or spiritual group has terms that define and label what they experience as *God*. These names for *God* all hold the same importance.

Because of the work that I have done with Native American teachers, the term that feels comfortable for me is *Grandfather*. Every day when I pray, I talk with *Grandfather*. Every day when *Grandfather* breaks through to my awareness, Ancestors and Angels accompany him.

The Ancestors, those whom I have loved and who have loved and continue to love me, show up. I *see* them: my Mother and Father, husband and friends, family and those whom I did not know in this life but who want the best for me. There are those whose shoulders I stand upon, those whose genes I continue to carry and those whose spirit continues to carry me.

There are Angels and Archangels who are absolutely everywhere. They want to support us. They show up. Archangel Ari'El has asked me to share these interactions because they aren't meant for me alone. Each experience recorded in this book taught me something important. Each telling of the experience is meant to model the possibilities for others, for you, to connect with Spirit.

Since I have begun this writing, I checked out other books about the Angelic Realm. One of my favorite Angel books is *The Physics of Angels,* which is a dialogue between theologian Matthew Fox and scientist Rupert Sheldrake. This is a must-read for those who are truly interested in the Angelic realm.

What I found amazing is the number of authors who are literally using the same or similar phrases: "The Angels have instructed, commissioned me to write this book now" (Lorna Byrne). "The Angels are underemployed, not called upon, stand around waiting for us to ask for their help" (Doreen Virtue).

Some of the best-known Angelologists are saying these things. I wondered: Why do I need to write this book if they have already said what I feel called to say? Recently my niece said to me, "Aunt Carol, you have to write this book because of your stories and experiences. People need to hear it from someone like you, too."

That's it! We need to hear the Angelic message from all kinds of people. We need to know that the Angels don't show up just for a select group. The Angels are here for all of us without exception. The Angels are waiting for us to open our hearts, our consciousness, to their presence. They are eager to meet us where we are on the spirit road. They manifest in a variety of ways.

When my niece, Jessie, suggested that I had a unique point of view, I hadn't thought about that. The Angels and the Archangels are insistent that these books be written. This book is one of the many stories that are begging to be told. NOW!

I remember a time when I was troubled about something. I called one of my spiritual teachers, Julie, who was an Ojibway Medicine Woman and an ordained Minister. She was an amazing woman. She taught me so much. I needed some help thinking the problem through. I called Julie. She lived far away in the northern wilderness of Wisconsin Julie answered her phone. After the usual greetings, I asked if she had some time to help with a troubling matter. Before I had the opportunity to say any more she abruptly stopped me. She said, "I don't know why you are calling me, when you are sitting in a *room full of angels* who would love to help if you would just ask them. They can't interfere. They can only respond to your request. So don't call me. Ask Them. You are surrounded." At that she hung up the phone and we were disconnected. I didn't know if I should be hurt by her apparent rejection or thrilled that I was sitting in a room full of angels with so much guidance at my beckoning!

That day was a turning point. I began to take seriously the presence of Angels and their deep desire to help if I would, if you would, if anyone would simply ask them. I kept all of this to myself because I thought that everybody would think I was crazy. I have learned that I do not have the right to keep these experiences to myself any longer.

Living in and with Spirit is a life filled with awesome adventure beyond my wildest dreams. This book is an invitation. Go for it!

CHAPTER ONE

First Vision: Meeting Aslan

My spiritual journey with angelic visions and communications began in a shocking, troubling experience. The tradition of Icon meditation led me to an experience that caused me to confront fear, confusion and discomfort. With a courage I had never known before, I pushed through this distress in order to come face to face with the ferocious and gracious presence of the Holy. Often in the Scriptures angels began their encounter with the words, "Do not be afraid!" This experience taught me how appropriate this reaction is. However, I did not get the comforting message not to be afraid; I had to confront the fear and pray through it. The result was a deepening of my openness to the fearsome and loving presence of the Angelic. The experience I will tell you now deepened my awareness of the Sacred and put me in touch with the fearsome and loving presence of the Angelic.

I was beginning my Doctoral Program in Spirituality at the Ecumenical Theological Seminary in Detroit, Michigan. I lived in Ohio. I traveled about three hours, nearly 200 miles, and stayed in the dorm to attend the week-long Intensive.

One of the first Intensives that I was required to do was called "Journey to Wholeness." In this week-long Intensive, we would start each morning with Body Prayer. This was a beautiful way to prepare the body for prayer and for the day's work by doing some gentle exercises and movement.

We would share a sacred writing, sacred text, a Rumi or Hafiz or other Mystic's poem. Following the reading we would sit in silent meditation for about 30 minutes. The Professor would call us back to real time out of the prayer trance. We would then share a little about that prayer experience and finish with a song and/or a simple circle dance. We would then share breakfast and return to the classroom for the morning lecture.

It was a wonderful mix of people: priests, ministers, rabbis, yogis, and more. Each of them brought a special richness to the gathering because of their unique points of view. There was richness because of the huge diversity. Being in Detroit was good because of the vast ethnic mix that surrounded us. The program was unique, very special.

The Dean was teaching us different prayer styles. One day, probably because we had an Eastern Orthodox Priest in the class, the Professor decided to teach us the use of Icons and Iconography for our prayer meditative practice.

We were studying Henri Nouwen's teachings about the use of Icons as a window to the Holy. It is not about worshipping a picture, but rather about a means to see through the image of the Icon into divinity. Icons are referred to as 'windows to the Holy.'

I had a rich background. I had been a Roman Catholic Nun for several years. I had learned a lot about this kind of prayer and meditation prior to this course. Most of the people in the room did not have the kind of familiarity and experience with meditation that I did. I thought, "Oh this is going to be easy, a piece of cake."

Our professor, Jack, placed an Icon of the Pantokrator on the windowsill with a candle on either side. Icons are painted with very specific colors. Each color has a unique meaning. For example, blue represents those things that pertain to heaven and Christ's divine nature. Red is the color of blood representing Christ's human nature. Gold represents uncreated light of God and Christ's inner light. Some of the Icon's features are enlarged or elongated to signify that the Icon receives information, hears our prayers. The fingers are long and pointing upward to direct our attention heavenward.

Jack invited us to center our focus, to move into silence by slowing down our breathing. With a few deep breaths, we began gazing at the Icon. Our assignment was to "gaze through it." After the fifteen-minute time we were to report on our individual experience.

When I was gazing at the Icon, a strange feeling came over me. The Pantokrator is the Ruler of All. I experienced this image as the stern Christ judging me. I thought to myself, "My gosh, that image of Christ is angry with me." I could feel a lot of anger pouring toward me. I became very uncomfortable. I took my eyes away, took a few breaths to clear the experience of such powerful emotion and started all over again only to have the same thing happen.

In desperation, I closed my eyes and decided that I was going to think of something else. I felt this huge anger coming through the Icon. I thought to myself, "This is crazy. I'm just going to close my eyes and imagine something else because I can't deal with this

Icon. Maybe it's just the style of the painting." I don't know what it was, but I felt so much anger that I became shaky and truly afraid.

I started again with my eyes closed. This time not only was the Christ image angry with me, but the image began to morph and change into a huge mouth with large teeth. This huge, tooth-filled open mouth was coming directly toward my face. It was so terrifying that I quickly opened my eyes and shook my head to get rid of the image and the feelings of deep dread and fear that were coming up in me.

No matter what I tried to do, my fear and discomfort intensified. I decided to approach this differently. I closed my eyes and pictured a different image of Christ. I no longer was looking at the Icon of the Pantokrator. I decided to picture the Laughing Christ, by Willis Wheatley. In this image Jesus has his head thrown back and he is enjoying a great belly laugh. Jesus is in total delight.

I closed my eyes replaying this image of Jesus in my mind's eye. For a fleeting moment, all felt safe. Suddenly the image changed; it felt like it was coming toward me. Jesus' mouth, opened in laughter, had morphed into a huge wide-opened mouth that was coming straight toward me.

It was no longer a human mouth. It had big teeth, animal-like teeth. They appeared as fangs and it was coming toward me. I began to panic and thought, "Oh my God, it's going to devour me." I opened my eyes and shook my head to get rid of the image, to get it out of my head. And I thought, "Whoa, what is the matter with me? I should be able to do this kind of prayer easily. What is going on?" This had never happened to me before, never, NEVER!

Then as I caught my breath from the intense emotion and fright, I wondered, what else could I do to create the portal or find the portal into this moment of meditation? I felt so pushed away, so put off. I did not understand and I was totally frightened. Every time I closed my eyes, no matter what I attempted to image, this ferocious face came at me and the same thing happened. I had to open my eyes quickly, shake my head to get rid of the image, because this mouth was coming to devour me.

My heart and soul silently screamed, "What is going on!" I looked around the room. Everyone else was in silent contemplation; yet here I was, the one with the most experience in contemplative and meditative prayer, struggling with this very simple assignment!

Before long the time was up and the Professor, Jack, was going around the room asking each of us to share something of our experience. My stomach wrenched. "Oh No! How am I going to talk about this?" Soon he came to me. Until now each one had reported his experience saying things like, "I was able to do it and this is what happened" or "No, I wasn't able to get past the Icon" or "No, it didn't mean anything to me or…." Everybody was sharing something.

I said hesitantly, "Well, this is crazy, but I'm going to tell you what happened." I shared with them just as I have shared with you,

After we all shared from our experiences, the exercise ended and we moved on to the next. Jack was setting up another prayer experience for us to "try on." No matter what I did that day, no matter what Jack asked us to do, I kept having that similar experience of something coming after me, and I was terrified. I simply could not close my eyes. I had never had an experience like this when I wanted to pray.

I questioned God, "What's going on? I don't understand this. I feel like you are pushing me away. Why in the world would you be pushing me away? You've always welcomed me in prayer. Didn't you tell us to 'pray without ceasing?' What's going on?"

I was really in a dilemma. It was so intense that during our break time when I was walking down the hallway, I was looking over my shoulder to see if something was following me that wanted to devour me. That's how real this experience was. My whole being was filled with fear, and I didn't know what to do. I had become very paranoid.

At the end of the day, Jack came to me and said, "I'm concerned about you being here alone tonight." He knew that I had driven nearly two hundred miles to the seminary. I was staying in one of the dorm rooms that the school provided for "out of towners."

Jack said, "We have a guest room at home. Would you like to come and stay with my wife and me tonight until you work through this?"

"No way," I said. "Not on your life. As soon as you leave here, I'm going back in that classroom, and I'm taking my chair and putting it knee to knee with that Icon." The Icon was positioned on a windowsill just above the radiator. "I'm going to sit with that Icon, and this time I'm not moving until I find out what's going on."

Jack said, "This has been a really hard day for you. Are you sure you want to do this by yourself?"

"Yeah," I said. "I've got to. I've got to get past this. I don't know what's going on. This makes no sense to me. I have to stand my ground and find out what's happening."

One of the other students, Doug, who had flown in from the East Coast said, "Jack, don't worry, I'll stay with her."

I said, "The only way that you can stay with me is if you stay on the other end of the room." This was a long classroom created by two rooms with the divider opened. "And you don't interfere, no matter what happens. You can't interfere because I have to get to the bottom of this."

"Okay, don't worry," said Doug. "I'll stay on the other side of the room. I won't interfere."

Jack said, "As long as I know someone is here with you, I feel better about you doing this on your own."

It was getting late. It was dark out now. We had our dinner. Everyone had gone home for the evening except for Doug and me. We went to the classroom and Doug said that he would stay at the other end of the room. I went as I described, knee to knee with the radiator. The Icon was sitting there with a candle lit on either side the way that Jack had positioned it. The only difference was that it was getting deeply dark outside, so the lighting was different.

There I was, preparing for meditation, changing my breathing to breathing more slowly, taking some deep intentional breaths, and I gazed at the Pantocrator Icon. As I gazed at the image, I said, "Now look, I just want to know what's going on and I want you to know that no matter what happens, I'm not moving. I'm not running. I'm not chasing you away any more by shaking my head. I'm going to sit here with my eyes closed in soft gaze until I know why this is happening and what is happening. I need to know what's going on."

I began my soft gaze, looking through the Icon as a portal to meet the Holy in prayer. Sure enough, here it came. It was coming at me with its huge mouth open. I could see the large fang-like teeth. I was hanging on to the arms of the chair with a tight grip. I was not moving!

"I'm not moving. I'm staying right here," I prayed in my heart.

It was coming right at me, and just as it was in my face, that huge mouth with the huge fangs closed. All I could see, because it was nose to nose with me, were two huge golden eyes. They were beautiful, soft golden eyes, intense. In my heart of hearts I heard,

"Now that I have your attention,
I want you to know how much I love you."

Overwhelmed with feelings of warmth, love, affection and deep care, my mind whirled and I thought, "Whoa!" The image was so close that I needed to back up to get perspective. I still did not know what I was looking at. As I pushed back it came into view. I saw the head of a huge Lion. He was beautiful! His eyes were deep and golden. His mane was full and thick. His nose was rich black and looked velvety. He appeared to be full of love and care. His gaze was one of tremendous tenderness.

In that prayerful vision, our sizes seemed to change with respect to one another. Most of the time I was very, very small, and he was extremely huge. His head was so much bigger than my body. It was unbelievably disproportionate. Then I seemed to be larger and standing in front of him. He took his tongue and licked my right side from the sole of my foot all the way up my side to the top of my head. I realized that I just got a Lion's kiss.

Now I sensed that I was smaller, and he picked me up on his tongue. He put me on the back of his massive neck in the soft ruff of his fur and let me lay there. It was warm, soft, and I felt protected. I knew that nobody could see me. It was like I was in tall prairie grass. I was so small in the hairs on the back of his neck that it was like being in a forest of fur. It was beautiful and peaceful.

The whole time all this was happening, the tears were flowing down my face. This was the most intimate lovemaking I had ever experienced. He was tender and caring and totally present to me. He absorbed me into his being, and in those precious moments he was all there was. There was nothing more. Nothing else mattered. Nothing else existed.

I have no idea how long I stayed with him. In a flash of reconnection with time and place, I remembered that Doug was at the other end of the room wondering what was going on. I had lost all sense of time and place and had no idea how long I had been sitting there.

I said to the Lion, "I am concerned that Doug is waiting for me. I really don't want to go. I want to see you again. Is that possible?" And he said, "Yes, you just have to ask for me."

Never having experienced anything like this before and being saturated in his deep love, I trusted that I would see him again. So I said my good-byes, my face soaked with tears.

I opened my eyes and started to push myself back away from the radiator and the Icon. I stood up and started to turn around when I realized that Doug was standing right there behind me. I had absolutely no idea how long he had been standing there. He looked at my tear-soaked face and asked, "Are you okay?"

I replied, "I have never been better."

I was different. I had changed from when I started. I felt calm, peaceful, loved and cared for. I told Doug a little bit about what happened and then we went off to our respective rooms.

In the morning as I came out of my room, the Prof was arriving for the day's classes. He came down the hallway and stopped to ask, "How did it go last night?"

"It was incredible," I responded. "I met this Lion."

Jack immediately said, "Oh, Aslan," and he walked away.

I quickly asked, "Who is Aslan?" but Jack was already heading toward his office. I stood there bewildered, "Who is Aslan?"

I had never read the *Chronicles of Narnia*. After this experience when Jack told me about the *Chronicles*, I read all seven of them. They are adult fairy tales about a Lion who so deeply loves the people and all the Land of Narnia that he gives his life for them. The Lion's name is "Aslan" and is called "The Great Lion." He is known as the creator and the one true king of the world of Narnia, and generally a figure of all that is good.

As we began a new day of teaching, I wondered how my experience of the previous evening would impact my learning and experience. Jack created another scenario in which we were invited to encounter Divinity in prayer. He taught about the prayer that Jesus shared in praying to "ABBA," which is an affectionate term in referring to God as "Daddy or Papa." Jack wanted us to feel the deep love and affection that God has for all of us as a loving Daddy has for his little children!

Jack shared the "Lord's Prayer," suggesting that we imagine "Daddy-God" as we nestled into God's lap in this time of meditation. I closed my eyes and began the deep breathing that we were taught as a way to clear one's mind and ground one's being in preparation for deep meditative prayer. I settled into my chair, breathed deeply and visualized the scene of Daddy-God waiting for me to nestle in his lap. I approached ready to meet "Daddy-God, Abba-Father".

As I approached I saw myself as young and quite small – perhaps two or three years old. I came to the side of the chair where "Daddy-God" was seated. I reached my little arms up as I felt the soft garment that draped over "Daddy-God's" lap. I pulled myself up, prepared to nestle into the warmth and love that a child knows when curled and wrapped in the love of her Father's arms.

Then a couple of realizations occurred to me. I noted that I had climbed into "Daddy-God's" lap and I had not seen his face. All I could see was this soft and welcoming space on "Daddy-God's" lap. What was more amazing was that the soft garment that draped "Daddy-God's" lap was made of fur. It was soft and held me just as the fur on the back of Aslan's neck had held and caressed me the night before.

It was in the experience and memory of the soft fur that I knew that the Lion I had met the night before and "Daddy-God's" lap were in fact the same presence. I also realized that "Daddy-God" would meet me where I am. "Daddy-God" was showing up for me in a new and vibrant way. The previous day I endured a deep struggle when seated before the Pantocrater Icon. The image had morphed into a "beast-like" presence with a large menacing mouth full of fangs and sharp teeth. It came at me as if it wanted to devour me. It seemed to me that this encounter was a turning point in my relationship with the Holy. I had never before felt the deep all embracing love and care of "Father, Abba."

The experience reminded me of Francis Thompson's Epic Poem, *The Hound of Heaven*. It felt like I had to experience the Hound of Heaven, the experience of being pursued by a fearsome God. I also experienced the push of Divinity. Both of these intense experiences happened over 30 years ago, yet I recall them as if they happened yesterday.

The outcome of this intense chase was necessary to prepare me for God's Divine embrace on the fur that covered "Daddy-God's" lap. The moment of being seated in "Daddy-God's" lap would have had almost no significance without the Hound of Heaven experience. The terror and fear of the hounding prepared me for the embrace of Divine Love, a love that surpasses all understanding.

The presence of the Great Lion has been with me for many years, ever since this vision in 1980. I have enjoyed numerous and diverse adventures with Aslan. Recently I shared this story with a friend. He enjoyed the read and then said to me, "You know that lion that you met is not Aslan. The Lion you met is a much larger presence than Aslan!"

CHAPTER TWO

Gort: Facing Fear

My spiritual journey and visionary experiences deepened with the study of dream work. In the Christian tradition, dreams are a common vehicle of sacred communication. Miriam, the sister of Moses, has prophetic dreams, as does Joseph--who also interprets dreams. In the New Testament, Mary's betrothed, Joseph, learns of the conception of Jesus through an angelic visit in a dream. In the Native American tradition, dreams are accepted as sacred visions. So, it is not surprising that the next step of my sacred experiences took me through the dreams of my childhood and adulthood.

My journey through the "dream-world" took a turn of depth and meaning through the study of psycho-synthesis, a fascinating dream work technique. It is a process of integration, which puts together elements of the unconscious, like dreams, with the rest of the personality. This was of special interest to me because my childhood dreams were problematic nightmares, which impacted my ability to remember my dreams.

For over forty years, I seldom remembered a nighttime dream. As an adult I wanted to solve this problem. I was bothered by the reality that others could remember and share what they dreamt at night and I couldn't. This class in psycho-synthesis was my opportunity to look at these childhood nightmares. I wanted to see if there was anything I could do to regain my ability to recall my nighttime dreams.

As a child I had a crippling recurring nightmare. I attributed this recurring nightmare primarily to watching the movie *The Day the Earth Stood Still* in which there was a humanoid robot named Gort, who had a single ray of light emanating from the middle of his forehead that could be a lethal weapon. Gort and his partner Klaatu were aliens; however, Klaatu looked very human-like. They had come as cosmic visitors to bring Earth a message.

Instead of taking heed and listening to their message, humans attacked and captured Klaatu, who was concerned that Gort was left alone. He was concerned that not knowing where Klaatu was, the robot might cause Earth catastrophic destruction.

As a small child I was filled with fear by this movie. Here is a report of my dream/nightmare: In my dream Gort showed up and absolutely terrified me. I saw myself about 5 or 6 years old, my age at the time the movie was released. In the nightmare, I was running from place to place. I was trying to hide behind different pieces of runway equipment, buildings and airplanes tires.

A huge flying saucer had landed. A ramp emerged from the bottom. A large silver Robot emerged from the flying saucer. I knew in my heart of hearts that if he caught me in the beam of his one eye's ray of light that he could trap me. He could "get me." In this dream I felt like he was pursuing me. Every night he caught me, and I woke up terrified with tears and cries. I was fearful that he was going to take me away in his spaceship.

Eventually because of this recurring nightmare my "dream machine" shut down. My conscious and unconscious mind worked out an agreement that went something like this: "This child is in a constant state of fear and panic that she is going to be abducted and taken away from her family by this humanoid Robot. Until this fear is resolved the two of us will no longer communicate during the dreamtime. Carol will not remember or recall her dreams until she can do so without being overcome with terror."

That agreement was buried deep in my psyche. It structured my life in ways that I never "dreamt" it could. It was an ever-present force. During my adolescence and into adulthood, this agreement stayed in tact to protect me from recurring nightmares. I no longer experienced the nightmare with Gort. However, the price I paid for the freedom from that nightmare was huge. I was no longer able to recall ANY dreams. It was due to my inability to recall any of my dreams that I chose to do my Doctoral Dissertation on the Spirituality of Dreams.

I longed to be able to remember my dreams and to have this valuable asset restored to my consciousness. Of course, I continued dreaming. It is a documented fact that everyone dreams several times a night. We must dream in order to be healthy and to remain sane; however, I no longer had any memory of my dreams.

I was a small child of six years old when my conscious and unconscious mind seemed to disconnect when it came to dreams.

All of my dream memory stopped for over forty years. Then I was an adult in this doctoral program. In a classroom filled with other students, I shared the reality of my childhood nightmare with the class. The instructor invited me to do some 'work' around this disconnect. I agreed. My hope was to move through and past the fear so that I could remember my dreams without terror.

The instructor used my condition of not having dream memory as a teaching opportunity. He introduced the class to some of the tools used in the psycho-synthesis approach to dream work. He took me through a pretty amazing process.

After what I experienced in this class, I decided to focus my dissertation on Dream Work as a spiritual practice so that I could help myself and others. My goal was not only for each of us to connect with our dreams, but also to learn from them. Personally, I felt so left out when people would talk about their dreams. I never had a dream that I remembered to talk about. This was the result of that one tremendously disturbing and recurring nightmare.

When the day's session was over and our work for the day completed, I went to my dorm room to prepare for sleep. One of the other women who stayed overnight in the dorm was very excited. I asked her, "What are you so excited about?"

She responded, "Are you kidding? I'm going to bed and into the Dream time; of course, I'm excited. I want to see what's going to happen tonight. It's kind of like going to the movies every night."

As I heard her words, I felt my longing. "Oh gosh, I wish I could remember my dreams." This nightmare not only impacted my dream life; it also impacted my waking life. Many times during those forty years I would experience fear in my daily life. I knew the fear was directly related to my nightmare.

Here are a couple of examples of how the dreamtime and the daytime overlapped. As a child, we lived in a two family home with my maternal Grandmother. My family lived upstairs and Grandma lived downstairs. One day when I was about ten years old, I went down to see Grandma. I walked into the front room alone. I "saw" a black figure that I called the "Tar Man." Although he did not look like the Robot, Gort, he felt a lot like him.

The figure was standing behind Grandma's couch with one arm raised. I knew that if I went close to him he would lower that arm to strike me. I was frozen with fear, terrified to enter the living room. I had to wait until others entered the room, and then I would feel safe enough to enter; however, I still "saw" him and felt his presence. I would not sit on the couch where I experienced his presence.

He appeared in similar stature as the Robot and his movements were robot-like, very stiff; however, he looked like he was wrapped in black tar paper. Even his face was wrapped in tar paper. I couldn't make out his face at all. The most noticeable features were the black tar paper and the raised right arm. That presence carried the same energy that the Robot did. I felt as though this thing was going to get me, cause me harm, take me away, and destroy me.

When I was older, probably in my thirties, I experienced this presence again. I was attending a private class in Transactional Analysis with Oswald Somerton in one of the students' homes. We met in their finished basement rec room.

Everyone went upstairs for a break and a snack of coffee and cake. Because I was busy setting up my microphone for recording purposes, I had remained downstairs in the rec room and would be joining them momentarily, EXCEPT, I couldn't go up the stairs. There was that same presence, the Tar Man, standing at the foot of the stairs, and I was terrified. He stood with his right arm raised and waited for me to attempt to climb the stairs.

My fear would not let me get past him. My friends were upstairs. They called down to me to hurry up and come up. I didn't know how to respond to them. I was frozen with fear. I simply could not go near the staircase. Then with all the courage I could muster, I made a dash for the stairs. I moved so fast that I tripped up the stairs. In my futile effort to get past the presence at the bottom of the steps before he could lower his arm, I fell flat on my face. These were familiar emotions. They were the same emotions as I experienced with the robot. I was afraid that he would "get" me and take me away.

My friends came running when they heard me fall face first on the stairs. I was so grateful that they came. I thought about feeling foolish, but that was fleeting. I was relieved and felt safe from the entity when they all came running. I wasn't concerned about the fall.

I realized from this experience that our nighttime dreams could also be our daytime fears. Since I completed my doctoral work I have facilitated numerous dream groups. I have helped all ages with their dreams, nightmares and night terrors. I have witnessed how the dreamtime infiltrates and can become a waking nightmare just as it had for me for all of those years.

There was one other experience that happened in the mid 1970s. This was not a dream experience; it happened in chronos time, real time. It took me a lot of years to realize that it is part of this set of dream and vision experiences. It is very different yet has a strong underlying theme that connects it especially with the Tar Man report.

Here is what happened: I was working as the Music Director at a church east of Cleveland. I taught and directed the choirs. The church building had an interesting internal structure. The wall behind the altar divided the large sanctuary from a small private chapel directly behind it. It was a shared wall. The Tabernacle, which was shaped like a gold box, held the sacred elements for Holy Communion. These elements consisted of the blessed bread that had not been consumed during the worship time.

When the Sanctuary was being used for something other than worship, there was a door that could be pulled in front of the Tabernacle. This was done to respect the sacrament, the blessed bread, that was housed there. Since we were using the Sanctuary for choir practice that evening it was customary for us to slide the door closed in front of the Tabernacle. I went up the steps and approached the Tabernacle to close the sliding door.

On the wall above the Tabernacle hung a Christ Resurrection statue. It was a hand carved wooden statue of Jesus the Risen Christ. It was carved out of wood and about four feet tall. Because it was a depiction of Jesus after the resurrection - rising from the dead – he was not depicted as crucified like so many statues; instead he was elated with his arms straight up in joy and freedom from death.

As I closed the sliding door I heard a cry, a gasp, from the members of the choir. Many of them let out a shriek just as I closed the small sliding door. Quickly I turned toward them to see what had happened. I thought someone had fainted or become ill. I found them all staring at me! I didn't have any idea what they were staring at. What had caused the alarm and the gasps?

Then they pointed and said, "Look at the Christ statue!" I turned around. I was still standing nearly underneath the statue, exactly as I had been to close the sliding privacy door. That's when I saw why they had gasped. They had witnessed the right arm of the statue move from its upright elated position and rotate down so that it was pointed to the top of my head. They had been fearful that it would fall off and hit me.

As I relive these events, I am aware of the uncanny similarity of my nightmare and this actual occurrence. As a child, I feared that the Tar Man would lower his arm and harm me. Here was the only time that it actually happened in chronos time. It happened in a way that there were numerous witnesses. It happened at the hand of one that I professed to love and I knew cherished me.

So then the questions started coming to me. "Was this a symbolic warning? Was this a symbol of selection? Was this a loving pointing out of someone who did her best to live a life of compassion and justice?"

I simply find it fascinating that what I feared would come about at the hand of a terrifying Tar Man actually happened in chronos time and space at the hand of the Beloved….and I never saw it coming. I didn't even know that it happened until after the fact. I knew the "dreaded" moment only because of the gasps of witnesses. Curious?

By the time I started working through these fears by selecting the doctoral course of study that I did, my life had been severely impacted by this childhood nightmare that lasted for over forty years. I was so relieved to finally find a way to process these deeply imbedded aspects of my soul.

When I first told the nightmare to my psycho-synthesis instructor and my classmates, I felt foolish. However, the deep process and what resulted during class that day was more than I could have ever hoped for. The process was powerful and the results effective. With the class gathered around me I laid on the floor covered up with a blanket to keep my body heat in, and a pillow elevated my head for comfort. The instructor then led me through a process that took me back in time. I went back into the dream, back into the nightmare. I relived the nightmare just as I remembered it.

I relived it just as I shared it with you, with all of the fear. I saw every piece of the dream as if it were for the first time. In reliving it, I experienced all of the fear as well. However, the instructor provided me with a structure that helped me to feel safe. Although I remembered and felt the fear, I didn't experience the terror that little Carol had had nearly 40 years earlier.

What was different this time was that the instructor used dream tools and suggestions that helped me to approach the dream images, especially the image that resembled Gort, the humanoid robot. One of the most important pieces of the process was when I was in the dream. The instructor suggested that I have a talk with Gort to find out what his intentions were. When he saw my fear, he asked what I would need to not feel afraid. Who could I ask to accompany me as I approached Gort?

Immediately, Aslan came to mind. I asked the Great Lion to be with me, and he was there as soon as I thought about him.

Having Aslan with me was critical to the success of this dream work breakthrough. Aslan stayed with me as I relived the dream. The Prof asked me to stay in the dream and to start moving toward Gort instead of hiding and running from him. I asked the Great Lion to be with me. He accompanied me to the ramp of the spaceship where the Robot, Gort, stood at least seven or eight feet tall. I have been terrified of this Robot for thirty-five years. I balked at the Robot's presence. Aslan said to me, "It's going to be okay. He is waiting for you. You go with him." These are telepathic thoughts.

Nervously I responded, "Only if you come with me."

He said, "No, you go with him."

I knew in my heart what the Great Lion was thinking. He knew that this was something I needed to do alone, that this was a time when I needed to experience and to learn something deeply that couldn't be accomplished in the presence of any other being, not even him. Perhaps, especially not him, since he protected me with a depth of caring. I needed to get over my fear of Gort's presence. This was one of the ways that Aslan shared his deep caring for me. He was so loving that he gave me the space I needed to have this experience.

Knowing that I needed reassurance, Aslan said, "I won't leave you alone. I'll be right out here waiting for you. You will be fine." By this time, I had spent significant time with the Great Lion and learned that I could trust him without question. When he said, "You go," I did. Now this doesn't mean I wasn't afraid to go. It means that even with the fear, because I trusted Aslan, I went.

In this waking dream I was the adult age of 41 years. Yes, I was afraid and yes, I went. Here' s how the waking dream unfolded: the Great Lion continued to encourage me to allow the Robot to approach me. It was evident that the Robot wanted to take me into his spaceship. Moving through my fear with the Great Lion next to me, I allowed the Robot to lift me up. He carried me like a child. He had one strong arm under my back and the other arm under my legs. He carried me inside the space ship where there were chambers that looked like the stasis chambers used for space travel in the film *2001 Space Odyssey.*

He placed me lying on my back in one of these chambers and closed the chamber lid, which is all glass. For a large metallic creature, he was very gentle in his movements. I was able to see through the glass lid of the chamber. I was apprehensive. He kept me there for a considerable time. During that time, I finally relaxed, assured that Aslan was waiting for me.

I felt like I was in another realm. I experienced a beautiful freeing sensation. When the experience was completed, the Robot opened the glass lid of the chamber and lifted me out. He carried me back outside and down the ramp. He returned me to the Great Lion. At this moment the Prof suggested that I ask Gort for a gift that was symbolic of his essence and his power. When I asked Gort for this gift, his huge frame began to melt. All that was left of him was a liquid metallic puddle. I actually felt a little sad. He had been so tender and kind to me. I knew, that he had given me the gift of his essence and his power in that gesture. I have come to understand that he is a part of me that is powerful and can be misunderstood as frightful. I need to hold onto my power and be gentle and tender as he was when I was afraid of him.

Since doing this Dream Work, I have not had any recurring fear or nightmare of the image of the Robot in either its metallic "Gort" form or in the Tar Man form. I have learned that every symbol in a dream, whether it is an object or a person, even a person that I know, is an aspect of my own self. Gort and Tar Man are the parts of my shadow representing my deepest fears that melt in the presence of my sacred strength represented by the Great Lion. Through these experiences I learned to trust Aslan, my sacred strength, explicitly. That's the way it was and still is with Aslan. He protected me in that Cosmic moment and he encouraged me then and continues to encourage me to learn and experience all kinds of awesome things. Some incredible things. Some unbelievable things. All true!

CHAPTER THREE

Silent Healer: Meeting Aztek

Working toward my Doctor of Ministry in Dream Work as a Spiritual Practice, I was making use of the dream work techniques that I was learning. Nearly every morning I would either go back into a dream that I recalled from the previous night or choose a dream that I continued to think about from another time. I began to notice that there was a unique man standing in the upper left corner of my vision. I decided to explore the meaning of this man, so I went back into a dream. It was in a wakeful state of consciousness. This process is called Active Dreaming.

The man that was showing up in the corner of my awareness had a distinctive appearance. He looked to have brown weathered skin and long black braids hanging in front of each shoulder. His grin was mischievous and somewhat toothless. He wore a denim jacket and blue denim jeans with black cowboy boots. On his head, he wore a straight brimmed hat with the very top missing. There was a large feather placed in the hatband at the back. His eyes were coal black.

One of the tools that I learned was to greet and connect with dream symbols as they present themselves. When I saw the man standing there, I thanked him for coming into my dreamtime and asked his name. He stood there and grinned at me. He didn't say a word. He simply watched me. This continued to be the case on subsequent journeys into Active Dreaming.

I was introduced to a Methodist minister who was holding drumming prayer circles in his home. This fascinated me. I wanted to know more about the prayer circles. I started to attend on a regular monthly basis. At the time I was having a medical problem that caused physical discomfort. I had seen the doctor and was advised to have some corrective surgery. I didn't want surgery. I believed that in many instances we could heal the physical issues that we cause in our bodies. So I began to explore alternatives to surgery.

With the surgery on my mind, I went to the Drumming Circle. We were checking in; a number of us had health issues to bring to prayer. The decision was made to share in a Healing Prayer Circle. The leader instructed us differently for this experience. Each of us placed a bandana over our eyes to prevent us from the influence of light and distractions. When he began to drum a steady heartbeat, we were to prepare ourselves for our personal journeys. He explained that there were three worlds to which we could travel: the Upper World, The Middle World or the Under World. He explained the differences between each of the worlds and why we would want to travel to them. This way of journeying is a Shamanic practice. In order to travel to the Upper World, I was instructed to imagine climbing a tree toward heaven or climbing a high mountain. The idea is to feel lifted up off the Earth and moving heavenward. I imagined myself climbing high into a very tall tree in our backyard. I lifted off from there. I was on my way to the Upper World where one seeks a healer.

When I arrived in the Upper World, it was incredibly beautiful. Everything glistened white. It was so brilliant I was amazed that my eyes could take it all in without discomfort or squinting. It was as if I was walking on firm clouds that misted around my feet with every step. I understood that there were seven levels. I wanted to explore all of them. The beauty of this first level made me wonder about the additional six levels. Were they the same or did each of them have a unique beauty? As soon as I began to look around, I noticed a man standing there. It was the same man that I had seen in my Active Dreaming sessions. He was dressed in the same distinctive 'Southwest clothing.' The man looked at me and said nothing. Here he was in the Upper World. For the very first time instead of his speechless grin, he indicated with a hand gesture that I was to sit down. I said, "I want to explore. It is my first time here, and I would like to look around. Isn't this the first of many levels?" Everything around me was pure white and cloud-like. I had learned that there were at least seven levels and some teach as many as ninety-nine. With eagerness I was ready to bolt.

Again he motioned to me to sit down. He was no longer grinning. He seemed quite serious. Although I wanted to persist in my adventure, there was a sense of urgency in his request. I sat down. He still did not speak. He indicated what he wanted with gestures. Then he asked me to lie flat on my back. This was the first time I saw him move from his standing position. He squatted down next to me and began to move his hands around my body without touching me.

Then he seemed a little perplexed. He was holding a cord of golden light! He seemed to be trying to figure out if he should send the healing light through me from the top of my head and down through my spine or from the base of my spine up through the top of my head. I chuckled a little at his look of consternation.

Finally he had the light moving down through my crown chakra at the top of my head all the way down to the root chakra at the base of my spine. Soon he had the golden light moving in a continuous golden elliptical pattern starting at crown chakra, down through all of the chakras, out of the root chakra and looping back up to start the pattern again, creating a continuous loop. He kept the light moving in an elliptical pattern for a while.

Now I knew why he was so serious about having me stay put. I looked at him and quietly asked, "Are you my Healer?"

He smiled gently.

"Would you tell me your name?"

He answered, "Aztek."

The rhythm of the drum became very rapid. We were called back from our journeys. I removed the bandana from my eyes as my consciousness reentered the room. I remained lying on the floor for a few minutes. I pondered what had just happened. I sat up and we each shared our experiences.

At the end of the week I met with the doctors for x-rays and to schedule my surgery. The doctors were perplexed when they reported that there was nothing to fix. They were a bit befuddled as they compared x-rays to a previous set. I didn't think they would be able to hear what I had experienced. I've learned that most medical doctors adhere strictly to a scientific medical model. Most would not be able or willing to accept my healing experience. I could only imagine their faces when I told them that I made a journey to the Upper World while listening to a drummed heartbeat; that I met an ancient Aztek healer who used a golden rope of light to heal me. I walked away with a smile on my face and a knowing in my heart. I had met my personal Healer, Aztek. I could feel his deep love for me. I felt privileged to include Aztek in my growing team of spirit helpers.

Since that time Aztek has helped me with various healing situations. One was very special. It taught me an incredible lesson, the difference between healing and curing. My Aunt Rosemary, with whom I was very close, was diagnosed with inoperable gall bladder cancer. She was being cared for at University Hospitals in Cleveland, Ohio.

I was living north of Detroit, Michigan. It was about a three-hour drive. When I visited her, I asked her permission to pray for her. She looked puzzled at my question. I shared that for me to pray for her without her consent would be similar to my coming into her home and beginning a cleaning campaign without checking with her first. She readily acknowledged that she would welcome my prayers.

Back home in Michigan, I had a room dedicated to spiritual practice and prayer. I had an altar set up in one corner of the room. I had a candle there to remind me of the presence of Divine Light when I prayed each day. There were other small sacred mementos that I had gathered in my travels; some small stones, seashells, and more. It was here that I practiced my daily meditation and lifted up prayers for those who had asked. I began an intense prayer regimen for my Aunt.

Every morning, I would visualize her lying in her hospital bed in front of me. As I prayed, I would see the six to eight angels gathering around her bed, each standing facing my Aunt. They had their hands gently holding her all along her left and right sides. Then I noticed Mother Mary come and stand at her head. My Aunt had a special devotion to Mary the Mother of Jesus. Whenever I visited her she would ask me to sing the Ave Maria. She found so much peace in that hymn. Then, Mother Mary was present. Gently, she held my aunt's head. I wondered at this scene of spiritual tribute and loving care.

Often I would have visions of the care that my aunt was receiving from Spirit. Each day when I called her, she would ask me what I saw that morning during prayer. One day, to my surprise, my aunt phoned me and asked, "Were you praying for me this morning at 9:16?" I thought it funny that she had the exact minute. I said I had been praying at that time. My aunt said that she could actually feel the prayers. I was surprised to hear this. Never had I heard anything like this before.

Because we seemed to be having a deeply intense prayer experience, we began to pay closer attention to what was happening. I started to keep track of the exact times that I prayed. When my aunt felt the prayer presence she would mindfully take it in. Later that day she would call and tell me the time period that she experienced the healing prayer. This went on for days. The experience of prayer for my aunt was a tremendous gift.

There was one afternoon that I had driven down from Michigan for a face-to-face visit. While I was there, the four of the Ursuline Sisters that my Aunt taught with at Saint Ann's Grade School in Cleveland Heights came to visit her. They massaged her feet with cream and blessed her with conversation, humor and prayers. During their visit they asked me to remain in the room, which I did. However, I knew it was good for my aunt to experience their visit to the fullest. I stepped back and stood against the wall of the room while they were tending to her. I went into prayer mode and was holding her in prayer when I noticed her eyes going around the room until she saw me standing back there. She locked eyes and smiled. I knew that in the midst of all of the Sisters, she was still able to feel the healing prayers I prayed with Spirit.

One day during my prayer time, Aztek came into my awareness. I asked him for further instructions. Should I call on my Aunt's healer to help during prayer time?

He said, "No."

Aztek stayed with me during that morning's prayer. When I needed to leave for work, I noticed that Aztek was very involved. I told him that I didn't want to leave, but I needed to. He told me it was fine for me to leave. He said he would stay with her and do the healing work himself. So day after day I prayed. Each time Aztek would be present. Just as he had used the rope of golden light to heal me, he was once again holding the radiant rope. This time he was holding my aunt side near the gall bladder and moving the light in and out as if to cleanse a wound.

This kind of cancer was reportedly extremely painful. The nurse had set up a morphine pump next to my aunt's bed. In the event of severe pain, she simply had to press a button and the morphine would enter her IV and bring her relief. One afternoon, Dr. Ellen Whyte, who was a personal friend of my aunt, came to visit. Being a medical doctor, Ellen looked over at the morphine pump. She noticed that my aunt had not used it. She asked why she hadn't been taking advantage of the pain medicine.

My aunt replied, "I thought that I was only supposed to push the button if I had pain?"

Ellen said, “Yes, that’s correct. So why haven’t you used it?”

My aunt said, “Because I don’t have any pain!”

Ellen looked at her in disbelief. Being a doctor she knew that my aunt should have devastating pain from this illness. That was my “AHA!” moment when I realized what Aztek was doing. We knew that the cancer was inoperable and irreversible. I never realized that he was creating a pain-free experience for my aunt.

One morning my aunt phoned and said that she needed to talk to me. She said that she knew that I would understand what had happened during the night. She wanted to know what I thought.

This was her story: Last night while she laid in the darkness of her private room, she felt some one touch her. She figured that the nurse had come in to check on her; so she said, “Hello.” No one answered and in the darkness she could not make out anyone in the room. She was about to doze off when she felt another touch. She opened her eyes, trying to see who was there, and asked at the same time, “Who’s here?” There was no answer. She closed her eyes and was just about to doze off again when she felt the touch on her chest near her heart. She said that in that moment she wondered what I would do in this situation. This is what she told me, “This time I did not open my eyes. I said, ‘I know you are here. Thank you for coming.’” My Aunt asked me, “Do you think what I felt was the brush of angels wings?” With tears in my eyes, I affirmed her realization: the Angels were close by, and soon she would be leaving with them.

Throughout the long illness, she NEVER suffered pain. Eventually her blood was poisoned by the infection, and her brain began to shut down. She went into a coma and passed away very peacefully: Healed! Though not Cured!

CHAPTER FOUR

The Guardians: One Chipmunk and Five Large Bees

In 2003 I traveled to my friend Julie's home to help her when she first moved into a new trailer that was built to accommodate her wheelchair. Julie and I enjoyed a warm relationship. Julie was Ojibway and one of my spiritual mentors. She had residue effects of childhood Polio.

I wanted to help her unpack her library by organizing and shelving her books. While I was there, she taught me through a powerful experience. While I stayed with her to help, she said to me, "I want you to go outside, walk down the road…" Now Julie's home is in the wilderness. The road is nothing but a dirt road with no cars on it. I don't remember seeing any neighbors while I was there.

Julie said to me, "You're going to get to some property just down the road a little bit. You'll know when you get there. When you do, I want you to go onto the property and to walk it. Now on this property, you are going to see the ruins of a house that used to be there and you'll know that you are in the right place. Just walk. When you finish, come back and we'll talk about it."

I said, "Okay, sure, I can do that."

Walking down the steps of the trailer, I turned left out of the area where her trailer was parked and walked down the dirt road. I came to the place that matched the description she gave me. As I turned to walk onto the described land, I removed my foot from the dirt road and placed it onto the grassy area.

Suddenly, I heard all this racket in the bush to my right. I looked over and directly at eye level there was a little chipmunk. He was squawking away. I never heard or saw a chipmunk do this. He was sort of chirping and making an entire ruckus; so I stopped and said, "Hello, little brother. Are you the guardian? Are you the gatekeeper? You must be. I promise. I come to do no harm. I just want to walk and see this beautiful land; that's all I want to do."

He wasn't buying any of that. He just kept going on, and going on. He caused quite a tirade. Every time I would take another step, he would start all over again. I would stop and I would talk to him. "Little brother, it's okay. I come meaning no harm. I promise. I won't do anything. I won't touch anything. I'll just walk."

I took a few more steps. As I did, all of a sudden, these huge bumble bees, really large bees, started bombarding me, aiming at my head. There must have been three, four, five of them and I thought, "Oh my gosh, now what?" I didn't know much about bees. I was a bit intimidated by their size, and I questioned their intentions. They reminded me of carpenter bees, and I wondered if these big bumble bees would sting me.

I didn't want to think about that. I just didn't think they would. I knew that yellow jackets will sting. I knew honeybees will sting; however, they only sting when the hive or they are threatened. I wasn't sure about these big bees. They were dive-bombing around my head.

I think most people would have been scared away by this aggressive behavior. The bees really didn't want me walking on this property. So again I said to them, "Brother Bees, I would really love your company if you would like to come with me. I mean no harm. I promise I won't do anything offensive. Why don't you accompany me and we will walk this land together."

I continued walking, and they eased up a bit; however, they stayed with me. They continued buzzing around my head while I walked.

As I walked, I started noting that it was a beautiful day. The sky was gorgeous. The sun was shining brightly. This was such a beautiful piece of property. It had some grassy meadows, some wildflowers and a lot of vivid Red Indian Paintbrush. As I walked, I became concerned. I was being very careful to avoid stepping on any of the wildflowers since I promised that I would come and do no harm. I didn't want to crush any of the flowers.

As I walked, and I was walking slowly, I turned around to look at the ground. In amazement, I could not believe my eyes and did not understand how this could be.

You would expect that a full-grown adult woman walking in this beautiful grass would leave some evidence of footprints. I expected the grass to at least be bent or an impression left where my size eleven foot had walked.

I was concerned about the flowers, but when I turned to look and see if I had done any damage there was no evidence that I walked there. None! The grass wasn't smashed. Every blade of grass was standing up and every flower was untouched.

It did my heart good. I was amazed; but it did my heart good because I said I came to do no harm and even in my walking, I was not harming anything. That really moved me. I mean my heart was so, so big with wonder and awe of this moment. At the same time I was so elated that I was keeping my word to the utmost. I came to bring and do no harm. I continued walking very carefully.

I heard a strange sound that I couldn't identify. I said to myself, "What in the world could that be?" At first I thought it was the sound of water running. I started walking through the field thinking that when I got past these tall trees I would find a flowing river. These were extremely tall trees with a canopy of leaves at the top.

Then, as I looked up, I noticed that what I was hearing wasn't water running at all! It was the tops of the trees as they were blowing gently in the wind. It was so beautiful. I could see them swaying and making this beautiful sound as the leaves caressed one another in the breezes at the top of the trees. It was gorgeous.

I continued my walking, and as I walked, I was purposeful to walk the boundaries of the property. I walked down one side and then turned to my left and walked across the back near the tree line. It was then I realized that I could see to my left in this large plot of land, the ruins of a home. There was very little left. I saw the remains of the house that had burned to the ground. There was a lonely pipe standing, probably it had been attached to the kitchen sink or perhaps it was part of the bathroom plumbing. There was a simple concrete square foundation outlining what had been the shape of the house. All of it was pretty much grown over with grass and weeds.

There were no ruins or rubble around the foundation. Nothing was left of the house except the slab foundation. I continued my walk and then doubled back so that I could walk past the ruins of the house and return to the spot where I entered the property.

When I got back to where I entered, the bees quieted down and stopped their aggressive behavior. I came to that little tree on the side, now to my left, and that little chipmunk was there. He was still giving me some of his squawkiness. I thanked him for allowing me to walk the land and for allowing me to see that I did no harm. I stepped off the property back on to the road, and the little fella quieted down.

I headed back to the trailer where my friend was waiting for me. She said, “So tell me, how was that?”

I thought, “Oh my gosh, how do I even begin to explain this experience?” I said to her, “What do you know about that property?”

She said, “I don't want to talk about it until you tell me what your experience was.”

I began to explain. I told her all about the little chipmunk who was the gatekeeper. I told her about the bees who were dive-bombing me, but I knew they didn't want to hurt me. They just wanted to deter me from coming onto the property. I told her about my voiced-out-loud commitment that “I came to do no harm.”

I told her about turning around because I might be damaging the wildflowers and seeing that there was no evidence of a footprint the entire time I walked the property. I told her about the rustling of the trees and thinking that it was water of a babbling brook only to look up and see the trees kissing, the leaves gently caressing one another.

I told her about seeing the ruins of the house and feeling the emptiness of that place where the ruins were. Then I told her about coming back to the spot where I had entered to say goodbye to the little chipmunk, and how as I stepped onto the road he became quiet and still. It was then that the bees left me.

And so, I asked her, "What is there that they are so busy protecting?" I already had a hunch.

She asked me, "What do you think?"

I said that I noticed that on the grounds to the right side some of the land looked like it was higher. It looked like *mounds*. I said, "Are those burial mounds?"

She said, "Yes. Those are Native American burial mounds and at least three families have tried to live on that property. Every time they build a house before it is even finished, it's destroyed one way or another: by fire, by wind, by whatever. It is always destroyed. No one has been able to live on that property. Those are burial mounds and the spirits do not want them disturbed."

I said, "So that's why they are so protective. Because of the ancestral spirits there."

She said, "Yes, that is why."

To be invited into this experience of Spirit, to see firsthand how the Spirits utilized nature all around me to communicate and protect what is sacred to them was humbling and appreciative. To have them accept my promise "to do no harm" and trust me in this holy sanctuary made me feel like being "inside" the vision of this altered reality.

I have been thinking about what I learned from this unique privilege of walking with the Spirits. After this incredible experience that informed all my senses and sensibilities, I pondered the importance of this experience for me. The ancestral spirits, the angelic beings, teach with purpose. What was their purpose? What am I to take away from this day of walking in two worlds? My answers might surprise you.

1. It is possible to walk in two worlds in a good way.
2. I can make my way through difficult unknown situations and do no harm.
   In fact, I am able to walk as a blessing, to bless as I walk.
3. There is much that I don't know or understand. All that is expected of me is to be open to learning and receiving the blessings of the unknown.
4. I have choices all along the way that can alter the outcome in significant ways.
5. There is much more to an experience than what I first encounter.
6. All of creation is divinely infused.
7. As I navigate this path called life, the challenges increase according to my ability to receive with openness.
8. I can manifest that there are humans who can be trusted with the mysteries of spirit.
9. In this situation intention was more influential than physical law. For example, my stated intention was that I would "do no harm." There was no evidence of grass or flowers being damaged as a result of my walking there. Physical law would have been evidenced in the weight of my footsteps leaving some imprint on the grass and damaging the wildflowers where I stepped. That was not the case. Nothing experienced "harm."

I invite you to jot down a list of learnings from this chapter. Perhaps you have an experience to write about. Discern your learning from it. Rushing through our lives we can miss the simple things that are deeply profound.

I imagine that the first Garden was witness to a harsh moment of turning away when God put a great Angel to protect the Garden forever. I was so privileged to walk this simple garden of wildflowers and home of ancestral spirits. I have no doubt that just as others who attempted to occupy that land were driven out, I could have been. I believe having an open and accepting heart full of respect and a desire to do no harm was my free pass into this sacred place.

I took away a great lesson of staying open and committed to the promise I make – to do no harm. Spirit knows our hearts and longs to trust us as much as I long to trust those who have gone before me. On whose shoulders do I ride? Whose life has enabled and empowered me to be who I am? Who of the ancestral spirits do I need to get to know better? How about you?

CHAPTER FIVE

Meeting Astro

Aslan terrified me before I could welcome and experience his presence in my life. "Gort" and the "Tar Man" frightened me in a profound way so that I could finally open up to the gifts that they had to offer me in the form of their personal essence and power. The fact that I wasn't even aware of what was happening when the statue of Christ lowered his right hand over my head seemed quite prophetic to me.

One day when I least expected it, Aslan was back, inviting me into an adventure. In another significant "waking dream," I am with Aslan, the Great Lion as you may recall. I met Aslan in my first vision experience. He telepathically speaks to me. I experience words or thoughts in my mind that I don't hear with my ears.

Here's what happened: In this "waking dream" or vision, Aslan, the Great Lion, carried me out into space. He lifted me up with his tongue and put me on a hair in his left ear. I was so tiny compared to him that I could sit up tall on this hair in his ear. I was very protected and kept warm by the fur of his left ear. We flew out into the Universe, into the Cosmos. It was an absolute delight. It was so much fun, such an adventure, and I just loved doing it.

We went up into the Cosmos. It was beautiful as we went up into the darkness and into the voids. All around us we saw gorgeous stars glittering and glistening. Aslan carried me up and up and up and up and out and out. The Cosmic dimension was huge. I have no idea how far we went and no words to describe the magnificence of the journey.

Through these experiences I learned to trust Aslan explicitly. That's the way it was and still is with Aslan. He took me out into the Cosmos to discover and to learn all kinds of awesome things. On this particular journey, he took me to meet someone who would be an important part of my Spirit Guide Team.

We arrived at a large platform out in space where there was a very large being. He looked like a super-human space man. Aslan introduced us. I was told that this being's name was Astro. There were times when I was unsure and hesitant. At those times, Aslan pushed me with his big soft lion nose to get me to go where I was afraid or hesitant to go. That was how he coaxed me this time with Astro.

Aslan gently pushed me with his nose and said, "Go ahead. Go meet him. You are supposed to meet him."

I said, "Okay." So I did.

It was a beautiful coming together. Instantly I knew he was very special and that we were going to have a unique relationship.

We spent some time together out in the Cosmos. He held me. I was transfixed by his stature and magnificence. After a generous visit of time and affection, Aslan brought me back through space and time to the reality of the moment. He brought me home. I have learned that Astro plays a major role in my personal self-esteem. I never know when Astro will show up. He often likes to surprise me.

Here is an interesting incident about one of his visits:

I was on my way to a job interview at Akron University. I was checking out a position to determine if it would be something I might be interested in doing. I parked my car on the street. I got out of my car and began to walk toward the office building where my appointment was scheduled. It was one of those days when my inner critic voice was giving me a very difficult time. I felt dumpy. I felt fat. I felt sloppy. I felt like this was not going to go well. I didn't know why I was there. I was just having one of those days when everything felt wrong.

As I walked from my car to the office where the interview was scheduled, all-of-a-sudden I realized that I was not alone. Astro walked next to me. I broke out into a full-faced grin. As soon as I realized that he was there, I felt ten feet tall. I felt beautiful. I felt on top of things. He has this way about him. He boosts my self-esteem. He helps me feel good about myself. Astro is this awesome presence that loves me so deeply that when I'm in his presence I can't help but love myself.

I went to the interview. I took control of the interview and had a fantastic time. I realized while I was in that meeting that I did not want this job. I decided I would have fun with the interview and then leave. The interviewer and I enjoyed a wonderful conversation. We had a good time. I let the interviewer know that I didn't want the job. Sometimes I wonder if that was the reason that Astro showed up, to make sure that I didn't go after a position that wasn't meant for me at that time.

After we talked, I was happily on my way with no thought about pursuing the position any further. I felt freedom in that decision. It simply changed the entire day to have this beautiful spiritual entity who loved me so deeply escort me into the building and let me get a reflection of the great love he had for me so that I could love myself in that moment. How special is that!

What was truly unique about this incident was that it wasn't a dream. It wasn't active dreaming. It wasn't a waking dream. It happened in chronos time. Astro walked with me and stayed with me during the interview. This was a truly unexpected and amazing experience of a spiritual entity's personal visit. Because of Aslan I have many of these special moments.

Aslan has taken me to incredible places and introduced me to entities that I could never imagine. He helped me to have these experiences. At times he literally pushed me past my comfort zone. Most important of all is that Aslan was always there, is always there. Astro seemed to be another aspect of Aslan and I know I can count on him also. I have learned from these experiences that my relationship with Aslan is one I can count on. No matter what.

There isn't a decision that I make that I don't first confer with Aslan. He is always part of my awareness. All I have to do is think about him. Sometimes I don't even have to do that. Sometimes he simply shows up – like Astro did – in a way that gets my attention and waits for me to notice.

In pulling these events together, I realized that night dreams, day dreams/waking dreams and actual chronos time events are all manifestations of Angelic presence and activity in my life. One of the most important things I learned about nightmares is that the fear and terror of the nightmare is to get my attention so that I can be aware and receive the blessing of the Spirit realm.

I don't, you don't, none of us needs to know anything about the process of being selected to do incredible work and share in divine feats. The Angels continue to arrive and work with us in many guises. You might wonder why they present themselves in so many guises. What I have come to understand is that they come in a way that each of us is most likely to accept. What I know is that if the angels had come to me in the form in which I now experience them in those early years, I might have missed the entire adventure. I know I wouldn't have been ready to receive them into my awareness. I believe that it would be highly unlikely that our daily working together as we enjoy now would even be a possibility.

CHAPTER SIX

Paul, The Little Boy and Buffalo

Being schooled in Counselling and Spiritual Direction, I often met with individuals in search of deeper meaning in their lives. Since meeting Aslan I knew that "schooling" wasn't something that happened only in a classroom. Aslan was putting me to school with daily opportunities that often came from encounters with those I counselled. Here is one of the memorable lessons.

Paul was a college student who had been coming for private counselling for over a year. For the sake of confidentiality, I have changed the young man's name. We shared a solid trust relationship. One afternoon, I was expecting him to arrive. I went to the door to find him looking very differently from his usual self.

He was a large, muscular young man. He was taller than I was. He was built extremely strong with a fullback stature. For his youth he had lost most of his hair and his complexion was rich and almond.

Usually he presented himself just as you might imagine a man of his stature might. He was proud and sure of himself. He was excited about life and eager to learn and grow.

On this day he looked very differently. He was tired and worn out. His left shoulder was bent forward. His back was bent, giving him a hunchbacked look. I was truly taken by surprise. Immediately I knew that something was very wrong. I was shocked to see him this way. I asked with gentle urgency, "What's going on? What is the matter?"

He looked at me with deep weary eyes and said that he didn't know what was wrong, but something was terribly wrong. I invited him into the office to sit and then we began the investigative journey into his obvious discomfort.

I used various techniques and discovered much as we traveled this seldom-traveled road. Often I have found that Spirit teaches me as I go. Through intuition and deep knowing, Spirit, Aslan and the Angels guide me.

As we explored together, he reported that he first felt strange a few days ago. I started asking questions to determine what might have triggered his apparent distress. All he could put together was that he did his normal things that evening when working for his dad at their inner city store. I asked him to go back and recall everything he did on the night that he thought he first started feeling strange.

Paul worked for his father. The family-owned business was in the old part of a large urban area. The building itself was very old and held many stories. It consisted of a main floor for sales and a basement for storage with a large walk-in-cooler. That evening while at work, Paul needed to gather some items from the basement. This was something that he did often. He reported that the basement felt strange. He did not like going down there, but he needed to restock the store for the next morning's business. He went down to gather the items needed from the cooler. He thought that was the first time he began to feel discomfort. He had been walking around with this discomfort for a couple of days before he phoned me for an appointment.

I had never seen anything like this before. However, I have this incredible support from spirit teachers. One of the strengths of my teaching and guidance work is that I help others to get in touch with their own personal inner guidance. I assist my clients in getting to know their spirit guides, their angels, by name and encourage them to work with their guides. They learn how to call on them, how to show gratitude, how to live with the knowledge of their presence and to trust their wisdom.

Paul already had these skills in place. He had a powerful animal spirit guide who had assisted him in the past. First, I internally called on my personal guides for instruction. Since I really didn't have a clue about what was happening with Paul, I knew that I would need to rely heavily on my trusted teachers and helpers.

Once I felt secure in their presence, I began asking questions and providing direction. This was our conversation.

Carol: Take a few slow, deep breaths and do your best to relax. When you are ready, summon your animal spirit helper. Let me know when he is here.

Paul's eyes are closed and there is a *quiet pause.*

Paul: Yes, Buffalo is present.

Carol: Thank Buffalo for coming. Pay attention to how your body is feeling.

Once you are in touch with your physical feelings, share what you are experiencing.

Silent Pause

Paul: It feels like something is holding onto my back and won't let go.

Carol: Where do you feel this the strongest?

Paul: Something is hanging onto my left shoulder.

Carol: Thank the presence for coming to you.

Paul: *addressing the unknown presence:*

Thank you for coming.

Carol: Ask, 'do you have a name?'

Paul, "Do you have a name?"

Carol: What does it say?

Paul: It doesn't answer.

Carol: Thank it again for coming to you and ask if it brings a message.

Paul: Thank you for coming to me. Do you bring a message?

Carol: Do you get a response?

Paul: No message.

Carol: Thank it for responding to you then ask what it is doing here. Does it need something from you?

Paul: It is so sad. It is crying. It seems like a little boy.

Carol: Ask him what he needs from you.

Paul: He says that he is all alone and afraid.

Carol: Ask how old he is.

Paul: He's seven.

Carol: Thank him for answering you, and turning to Buffalo, ask what you need to do next.

Paul He says that the little boy needs to move into the light.

Carol: Ask Buffalo how to get the little fella to let go of you.

Paul: He says to tell him about Buffalo and that he is going to get to ride him.

Carol: What does the little one say to that?

Paul: Buffalo has already moved in and is getting the little boy on his back. He has explained to him that he is going to be with his family and friends and doesn't have to be alone anymore.

Silent Pause

Carol: What's happening?

Paul: Buffalo is walking away with the little boy on his back.

Carol: How are you feeling?

Paul: Free!

Carol: Thank the little one for taking the ride on Buffalo. Thank Buffalo for his wise counsel.

Paul: I have.

Carol: When you are ready, say goodbye to them, take a deep breath, and gently open your eyes. How are you feeling now?

Paul: Wonderful!

Carol: Is there anything on your back now?

Paul: No. It is completely gone.

Carol: I thank all of our teachers and guides for directing us through this experience.

Paul: Whew!

When our time together was completed, Paul was quite exhausted. I encouraged him to get something to eat before driving home. Eating some food is a good grounding after being involved in such a deeply spiritual encounter.

Thank you, Aslan, and all of my teachers and guides for continually teaching me. There is no school anywhere that could teach me the depths of what you teach me.

CHAPTER SEVEN

A Great Archangel Walks Behind

Angelologist, Doreen Virtue, was invited to do a weekend workshop at El Paso First Christian Church where I was pastor. I had never met Doreen before. Her business manager accompanied her in. She was waiting for me in the parlor. The parlor was a very large room. It was the equivalent length of two rooms. The parlor was beautiful with rich furnishings. The windows were intensely colored contemporary stained glass that glistened in the Texan sunlight. The floor was densely carpeted. There were several plush couches, end tables and more. Doreen Virtue was sitting at one end of the room on one of the couches. Members of her team and members of the church team were milling around, getting acquainted.

I walked into the room from the door on the opposite end of the room. I could have been anybody from the Church. I was not wearing any distinctive clothing or symbol, nothing that would alert her to the fact that I was the pastor. As I walked toward her, Doreen Virtue looked at me and said, "You must be the pastor."

I said, "Yes, I am." I wondered how she would know who I was with such certainty. We all looked the same as far as I could tell, so I asked her.

Doreen said, "I could tell because of that huge Archangel that's walking behind you."

Her comment made me pause. No one has ever told me that there was a huge Archangel walking behind me. Skeptically I said, "Really? Okay." What I knew in an instant was that it was Aslan. What I have come to understand is that Aslan's essence manifests in different forms depending on who is witnessing his presence.

There are times when I feel his huge Archangel's wings wrap around me in protection. There are also times when I feel his huge wings wrap me in loving embrace. There are times when Aslan the Lion sprouts wings and becomes the flying Lion. Most of the time when he carries me out into the Cosmos to teach me something, he positions me for our journey on a hair in his ear. Obviously at those times, he appears as a huge lion and I am extremely small during the journey. Once in a while, he lifts me on to his back. His size is smaller so that I can straddle his massive neck with my legs and hold on. Most often I don't see or experience his wings. We simply go airborne and fly seemingly by will or intention. But there are times that I also see him as the winged Lion.

Aslan manifests in different ways depending on the circumstances of the moment. What I've learned is that it doesn't matter. I can tell by how I feel that it is Aslan. All that matters to me is that it is Aslan. I know that I can trust him with my life. I know that he wants the best for me and that when he is around, which is all that time, I know I am protected.

Within a month after meeting Doreen Virtue, I traveled from my home in El Paso, Texas to Point of Vision Presbyterian Church in Royal Oak, Michigan. I had been invited to lead a drum building retreat. I have long been a builder of Native American single sided hoop drums and have led retreats in many locations around the country. I arrived at Point of Vision Church to lead this drum building retreat. I prepared the space in the circular form of the Medicine Wheel with Creator at the center. There were candles marking the four cardinal directions. I blessed the area by cleansing it with the smoke from burning herbs sacred to Native People. In this way, the space was made ready for those who would be joining me to build their sacred drum.

As participants arrived, they were asked to congregate in the hallway outside of our designated space until all were gathered. When everyone was accounted for, I explained smudging, a ritual of cleansing and blessing that used smoke from the burning of special herbs. The herbs used in the smudging ritual were sweet grass, sage, cedar, copal and lavender. Each one was smudged as they entered the prepared and blessed space.

They were instructed to walk into the Sacred Circle moving clockwise around the circle, paying attention to how they felt as they walked. Each one was directed to make at least one complete circuit around the circle before selecting a place to sit. The selection would be more about the circle calling them to a place rather than each of them choosing a place. They did this, and each one found her place.

Once they were settled, my plan was to open the Circle with a ritual that would prepare them for the sacred work of creating a drum. Creating a drum is sacred work because it is the way one connects with the heartbeat of the Creator, of Creation, of the Cosmos. At that very moment, with all of us standing in our places around the Circle, one authoritative voice spoke out from the group, announcing that the Ojibway Tribal Council had sent her. She asked me, "By whose authority are you teaching this Circle and Drum Building?"

I saw a woman small in stature and large in presence accompanied by a younger woman. This was most unexpected. I paused and addressed her. Immediately, I gave her a gift of tobacco, which is an honoring custom. She requested a list of my teachers and asked by whose authority I was teaching this drum building class? I shared with her my list of teachers. I explained that Jorge Arenivar, Red Tail Hawk, Tarahumaras Indian of Northern Mexico had taught me to build drums. Jorge (Spanish pronounced *HorHay*) had strongly encouraged that I teach others to build drums.

When Jorge had suggested that I teach drum building, I protested that I couldn't teach others to build drums because I was not Native American. Jorge laughed at me and said, "You are Native Spirit and you need to be teaching others to build drums." I finished up my second drum with him and returned home. I had not said anything to anyone about this encounter. I really had no idea how I was to do this. I was not even sure that I wanted to teach others to make drums.

Jorge told me that he couldn't possibly teach everyone to build a drum and everyone needs a drum in order to be in sync with the heartbeat of Creator. He said that I would be able to reach people, especially white people, who might not come to him to build a drum. I had built a couple of drums with Jorge, Red Tail Hawk, and I loved building them; however, it was an extremely difficult process.

As the Universe does, within two weeks of this conversation with Jorge, I received invitations from two different groups to come and lead a drum building retreat. This was over the top strange. One would have thought I had advertised that I was going to lead drum building retreats. Truth be told, I had not mentioned anything about this to anyone.

I have worked with people in several states and continue to teach drum building as invited. I always do it in a way that would show honor and respect for Native teaching. I keep the Native American way of never charging a fee for the sharing of spirituality. I only ask for the cost of supplies and the preparation fee for cutting the hide and punching the holes and whatever other supplies are needed or rent that needs to be paid for space. If after the day and a half together someone would like to make a love offering for the teaching, I will accept it – but it is never expected.

Back at Point of Vision Church in Royal Oak, Michigan, responding to the Tribal Council's request, I completed sharing my list of Native Teachers – which of course I had to pull off the top of my head. The Native representative, Annie, then pulled out a scroll that she opened and began to read to all of us a list of her ancestors and teachers. When she was finished, I realized that the encounter had taken about 45 minutes of our class time. I suggested to her that SHE open the circle since she was the Native American guest visiting us. She declined and said with the same authoritative presence, "You open the Circle. You are the Teacher here."

I was rather amazed after the encounter to hear her suggest

that I continue with opening the Circle. After I opened the Circle, I had everyone begin their process. I walked over to the two Native American women. I now realized that they weren't registered for the weekend. Annie immediately said to me, "I'm so sorry that I had to do that. I knew you were okay from the moment I saw you with that huge Archangel walking behind you, but the Council asked me to come and speak to you."

Needless to say, at that very moment I stopped when I heard her words, "…that huge Archangel walking behind you…" It hadn't been but a couple of weeks earlier and nearly 2000 miles away that Doreen Virtue had said the identical thing to me. Then I wondered, "Is there a huge Archangel walking behind me?" This experience is what triggered my thinking about Aslan's true identity. I knew he was very special. It seemed from these two separate reports that those who see angels can actually see him behind me! I felt his loving presence and his large, enfolding wings around me in a protective, caring embrace. Sometimes I can feel myself leaning back into his presence as he holds me.

After my first vision experience of meeting Aslan, I learned to use active dreaming to meet him again. I prepared myself by quieting my body and my mind with slow deep breaths, just as one prepares for prayer and meditation. I asked him to come, to make his presence known to me. He did. It was this incredible coming together of ageless friends. I don't know how else to explain it. It was like we had known each other and been together since the beginning of time. I did not know exactly how to talk about whom or what he is. I used to think that he was actually the face of God for me, since my "Imago Dei," my Image of God, the way that I understand God, had evolved so much over the years. I know that the "Face of God" is everywhere in Creation. I hold to the panentheistic teaching of God being in everything and everything is in God and God is more than everything!

What I realize now is that Aslan is a very special Spirit presence. He is part of the divine whole of the Holy. There are many sacred ones that are part of the whole of the Holy. Here is a way of understanding this that works for me. The Ocean is made up of kazillions of raindrops. That's how it is. You can take one little drop out of the Ocean, but it longs to be part of the Ocean because it is when they are together, the one drop and the Ocean, that they are what they are in full potential.

There are times when the Ocean allows some of the drops to individuate. For example, there are times when the waves roll on to the beach and become droplets on the sand. There are other times the Ocean gives up some of its droplets to become mist or fog. Each individuation is followed by the possibility and strong probability that the one drop will reunite with the Ocean. That's how it is with Aslan. He is part of the whole of the Holy and when I need a way to communicate with that vastness of beauty and Spirit and knowing which is the whole of the Holy, Aslan, the Great Lion, is the way that has been provided for me to do that.

CHAPTER EIGHT

A Royal Procession of Angels

Damanhur is the most magical place on Earth that I have visited. The community that has gathered in the beautiful Valchiusella Valley near Turin in Northern Italy possesses the rare ability of being able to not only think outside the box but also to act on the ideas and dreams that they receive. What they imagine, they create. They are a people who believe that anything they dream can materialize through the hard work of their hands and the spirit of creativity. See: www.Damanhur.org

I accompanied a group of Wisdom University Doctoral students to Damanhur for a learning intensive. Damanhurian Esperide Ananas was our guide. She invited us to a classroom for teaching followed by participation in a "guided meditation." Esperide began by sharing with us amazing Selfica Technology. Through study and experimentation, scientists and technicians at Damanhur have developed Selfica devices. The devices conduct and concentrate healing and intelligent energy that is available all around us. This healing and intelligent energy can be shared with our human consciousness.

The Selfica that Esperide held was about the size of a circular dinner plate. The device was piled high with copper wire in spiral like twists to a height of about five inches. In addition to the copper, the device was made with alchemically prepared liquids and more. This technology was believed to exist in Egypt and other ancient cultures.

After her teaching we were asked to stand and move our chairs to the walls. When the space was cleared, Esperide placed the Selfica on the floor in the center of the room. We were instructed to lay down on the floor, forming a circle around the Selfica with our heads to the center and close enough for our arms or hands to touch. There were twenty-four of us. We situated ourselves in the requested formation, lying on our backs on the floor in the close knit circular formation.

As in any guided meditation, we began with slow, deep breaths, relaxing our bodies and quieting our minds. She proceeded to lead us into a meditation that was truly "out of this world."

Esperide began by asking us to imagine the circle of our bodies as a large spaceship. She then suggested that our spaceship spin in preparation for takeoff. As we spun, our spaceship lifted off, and we began our journey into the Cosmos. To be honest, after we lifted off, I heard very little of Esperide's voice. I was thoroughly engrossed in the meditation and soared through the vault of the heavens.

Aslan, the Great Lion, manifested. He asked me to ride on his majestic back. I was seated forward on his back close to his neck. His size changed dependent on the nature of the vision. In this guided meditation he was large, and my size was proportionate so that I straddled him at the base of his neck, much like one rides an elephant.

I rode Aslan. He was so stately and proud. I was filled with magnificent joy to be with him like this. I felt so honored and special. The moment was radiant with power. My Spirit Healer, Aztek, walked to our left. He looked up and said to me, "Carol, turn around and look."

I was engrossed in the intensity of the experience. Everything about it was stately and regal. Simply being seated on Aslan's back was an incredible experience. With his large smooth strides, he glided into a village. I felt so Prince or Princess like. So Royal! I felt like a Queen. Aslan was so utterly magnificent. To be riding on his back as he carried me into the village was a feeling beyond exclamation. I thought that Astro and Aztek were the only ones there with us.

Once again Aztek said, "Carol, you need to look behind you."

This time I listened to Aztek. From my seated position on Aslan's back, I turned to look. Behind me I saw a scene that overwhelmed me, literally took my breath away. The most glorious thing I have ever seen. It was beyond my wildest imagination.

There were thousands, maybe millions, of ANGELS following us. Some seemed to be walking and some seemed to be flying. Multitude upon multitude of Angels followed us. I became acutely aware of the reality of the moment. I was on Aslan's back leading a procession of Angelic beings! My heart jumped in my chest. I was filled with feelings of awe and majesty, *doxa* and glory.

The entire experience was breathtaking. I was amazed then and every time I recall the images. I find the memory fills me with the same awe and wonder as I first experienced.

After a while the guided meditation came to a close. Our spaceship was spinning in for a landing. We came to a stop on the floor.

We were invited to share our experiences. I wondered since we became the spaceship together if our experiences would bear any similarity. That was not the case. Each person's experience was uniquely different.

Ever since then I have wondered if the Selfica had anything to do with the vibrance or the content of that experience? I have run out of words that can describe it.

What I do know for certain is once again Aslan showed up and treated me to a tremendous experience beyond my wildest imagination.

Today I am rewriting this experience in an attempt to share the depth and breadth of it. My body is alive in the memory of this scene as if for the first time. My torso is tingling with a familiar awe, and my mind exclaims, "Yes, this is where I live!" The energy that filled the first experience did not end in the telling; rather, it is revisited in each remembering. Every time I share this moment I feel it in my skin, my body, my heart, my mind.

My heart of hearts is vibrating with the excitement and the acceleration of immense joy just as in the very first experience of being surrounded by such magnificence. I feel the angelic realm holding me and lifting me. I know that my presence, here on Aslan's back, is important to the completeness of this moment. This eternal moment has no beginning and no ending. This moment continues in me right now and every time I recall this scene. What I know is that this is not some scene out of a story book. This is the reality in which my soul lives. I am challenged to acknowledge this magnificence as my reality and not just something that I am permitted to gaze upon.

This is the essence of these chapters, the reason Ari'El and I are sharing these experiences with you. You are invited to live this same soul life. Everyone is invited. There are millions of angels waiting for you. Come and meet your Angelic guide and I promise your life will never be the same.

CHAPTER NINE

Coming on the Wind

One morning when I was at the Recreation Center where I go to work out every morning, I went to my prayer place at the resistance pool. The resistance pool is an area set apart at one end of the swimming pool. It is circular and the water jets move the water in a counter clockwise direction. I pray here every morning before joining my friends in the leisure pool for my water aerobic workout.

That morning I was walking in the resistance pool by myself. I was talking to Grandfather (name comes from my Native American association with God/Creator) and to the Ancestors (those who have died before me) and to my Mom and to the Angels.

I said, "You know, I'm really having a hard time. I need some help." This was already October-November. Mom had died in August. I was still crying regularly every day and just could not get my act together.

I prayed, "I have so much that needs to be done and I'm not getting it done. I really need to get on with my life. Can I get some help with this?"

I heard this message from Grandfather in my head and heart, "You know how I come to you on the wind and give you a kiss with the wind's breath?"

I said to Grandfather, "Yes, sure, I know how you do that."

Grandfather said, "Just as you receive kisses on the wind, your Mother is going to come to you on the wind."

I thought, "Okay, whatever that means." I had no clue what that meant. I concluded my prayer time and went over to join my friends for the water exercise that we do each morning. When I finished my usual routine, I left the Recreation center and came home. Once again I was in tears, simply having a hard time with the depth of my grief. I was pacing. My friend Christopher was in the kitchen. He caringly said, "Why don't you go outside…"

It was a beautiful fall day, crisp and cool. The sky was so blue, the sun so bright, just a few little white clouds, a magnificently beautiful crisp fall day.

Christopher said, "Why don't you go out in the backyard? Get your prayer bench. Sit out there and pray. Get yourself grounded."

I said, "Okay, gotta do something, cause this is just killing me, walking around crying all day." I picked up my prayer shawl. I needed the comfort of my prayer shawl, and it would keep me warm on this crisp cool day. I went outside. I set my prayer bench in the backyard facing East because the sun was rising. I wanted to feel the sun on my face. It wasn't yet noon.

The sun was so warm and shining brightly on my face. It felt good to be wrapped in my prayer shawl. I was out there on my prayer bench. In front of me as I was facing East was beautiful old Grandfather tree that I loved very much. I know that we have a deep spiritual connection. He was one of the reasons that I bought this property. Instead of buying the property for the house, I bought it for the trees! He was one of the trees that really called to me.

I was sitting there talking to old Grandfather tree and to the spirits of the place who are always there for me. "I really need some help. Please help me move through the grief so that I can go into the house and get something done." Then the noise started. It was so strange. At first it was very soft. I wondered, "What is that noise?" Usually, I am very good at identifying things, but this was a noise that I did not recognize at all. I could not even figure out where it was coming from.

The whole time I was sitting out there in the beautiful sunlight, there was stillness. The sky was radiant blue. The air was crisp, cool. I was looking at the enormous Grandfather tree. He was so tall; the tallest tree in the yard. And I heard this noise. I was trying to figure out what was going on. I could not see any reason why there would be any noise. It started rather slowly, then intermittently kept getting louder. It grew in intensity and sound. It became more continuous until it was a constant sound. I was truly perplexed. "What was that noise?"

Finally, I turned around. Behind me there were trees nearly as tall as Grandfather. Some were next to the back fence and some were in the neighbor's yard. The trees were blowing so hard that their tops were bending, and to be honest I was scared. Those trees were bending so severely that it looked like they were going to simply crack their branches and fall. I turn back around to face old Grandfather tree. He was not moving! Not one leaf was moving!

I turned to look behind me again, and all of the trees were waving in a fierce Wind. Then the realization came to me. It was as if a light bulb turned on inside of me. I recalled what the Spirit of God said to me in the resistance pool that morning: "Your Mother is going to come to you on the Wind."

I cried out, "Oh My God! Look at those trees!" Tears streamed down my face. These were new and very different tears; tears of fright, tears of joy, tears of elation, tears of grief, tears of amazement! I recalled Spirit's words once more, Whoa!

"Your Mother is going to come to you on the Wind."

Then I laughed out loud and shouted, "Mom, what an entrance!" I was totally amazed! I saw all of the huge trees bowed to nearly breaking and behind me Grandfather was not moving even one leaf.

I ran into the house. "Christopher! Christopher, come and look at this! Come and look at this!" It was such an amazing sight to behold; utterly and beyond all doubt. Amazing! What was happening, could not happen, but it did!

I remembered Christopher's smile as he began to connect with the fact that something truly out of the ordinary was happening. Then I remembered, since I had forgotten about the morning prayer message from Grandfather at the resistance pool, I had not shared that message with Christopher. When I ran into the house and exclaimed to him the marvel of the Wind in the trees, he had no clue about the much deeper implications of this highly unlikely physical reality.

It was in that auspicious moment that I told him about my morning prayer experience and message. I shared the import and impact of what was happening on the spiritual level in addition to the marvel of the physicality of this "impossible" event, and Christopher's smile broadened.

Immediately, I went back outside to my prayer bench and took all of this to prayer. Instantaneously Aslan showed up, like he always does. He comes when I reach out for him and he comes when he reaches out for me. He is actually with me all the time. All I have to do is make myself aware. I know he is right here. Like right now: "Hi Aslan."

Aslan is really happy that I am writing these stories to share with you and others. He wants everyone to know that each one of us has the opportunity to work with angels. Each one of us has a guide angel, an angelic coach with us at every moment of our lives. It is not an extraordinary experience to feel an angel beside you. For those who open and trust and allow – the angels are at our side always. They want to be of help and want to help make our lives full.

On that day of Wind and wonder, I was fully aware of the fulfillment of Grandfather's early morning prediction. I knew that my Mother had truly come to me on the Wind. I spoke to Aslan in the vision that happened all around me. The Wind had quieted now but the energy of that physical, turbulent expression continued to tingle the air.

I asked Aslan about my Mom. "How is she?"

And he said, "She's right here. Do you want to see her?"

I said, "Oh, I would love to."

He brought my Mom into my awareness, and I could see her. She looked so beautiful, so radiant. I noticed that she was not alone. There was my dad. There was my husband. The three were all good friends when in the body, and it seemed that they continue their friendship in spirit.

Then I saw more and more of the Ancestors and family members. They were gathering in a slow processional. They came and encircled my Mom. So many. There were so many who have gone before me and there they were. There were so many gathered that I could not count them. They were gathered in concentric circles around my Mom. It was as if they were performing some sort of ritual welcoming of Mom while I looked on. I was standing there. I smiled at her. I felt incredibly grateful to see her so happy, so radiant, so held and so deeply loved. It was such a beautiful meeting of all of the Ancestors.

Aslan stood with me. A prayerful powerful moment! It was not a moment for words. It was a moment for Being. It was not a moment to Do anything. It was a moment for Seeing. It was a moment to stand in the radiant presence of Divinity and know the fullness of silence. It was a moment of huge divine love all around me and I wept. I wept tears of quiet joy, contentment, peace. My heart full, I sighed… Thank you, Aslan.

CHAPTER TEN

Archangel **Ari'El**: The Lion of God

Every morning, as is my practice, I go to the resistance pool around 7:30 a.m. Over the years, people have come to know that I go to the resistance pool for quiet and prayer. They respect my alone time.

When I first started this practice the lifeguard would come over to visit. He wanted to strike up a conversation. This was a thoughtful gesture, but I wanted solitary quiet for meditative thought and prayer. Finally, I said to him, "Did you know I come here to pray in the morning? I would appreciate it if you could check on me from the other side of the pool. If I need your help, I promise I'll wave."

He got the message. He left me alone in my personal stillness. My swimming friends also understood and honored my solitude and prayer time. The first 15-30 minutes that I am in the water people generally refrain from starting conversation and leave me alone. Because I am permitted this alone time, an extremely beautiful thing happens. Each morning when I come into the pool, I walk directly toward the resistance pool. As I approach, before even getting into the resistance pool, I sense a beautiful loving embrace, and I hear Grandfather in my heart saying, "I love you." My heart jumps for joy. I feel like a little kid going to see her nurturing Grandpa. When I actually enter the resistance pool, I jump into the strong counter clockwise current, lift my feet off the bottom and imagine Grandfather is spinning me round and round in the pool.

Have you ever had the experience as a child where one of the adults would stand behind you, pick you up by holding onto you under your arms and spin you around? That's how I feel in this pool. I feel just like a little kid that Grandfather is spinning around. It's a joy-filled love dance.

After I spin around a couple of times I begin to focus on my thinking. I notice that I do a continuous rant of unimportant trivia. I dump everything out of my head that I want to let go of. Lately, I am learning to simply say, "Okay, I'm quieting my mind and I want to listen." There are mornings when Grandfather and I have a vivid conversation. I think, if anyone is watching me, they think I'm absolutely loony because I know my mouth is moving. I actually talk quietly aloud. Sometimes responses come quickly into my head, quicker than I can formulate my questions. I have a big smile on my face because it is amazing to have this kind of conversation. It is fun. Often I am filled with the delight of the spirits that gather around me.

When I get into that water, into that pool, Grandfather is always there. Grandfather is the first to greet me with great love and acceptance. Once I greet Grandfather, my awareness expands to the others who are there. I welcome and often talk to my Ancestors.

There are those that I know, my mom and my dad, my husband, grandparents, other family and cherished friends and those that I don't know. I invite and welcome those whose shoulders I stand on who solely want my highest good and what is best for me.

Then I bring my attention to the angelic presences and welcome them. Archangel Ari'El is very present and the others are less distinct, however, truly present. Often I will ask for specific help for the day and the tasks that I know I will be engaged in. I have asked the angels who know art well to guide me in the design of the cover art for this book. This is of critical importance since I am NOT an artist.

About a year ago, I was in the resistance pool floating around on the current. On this particular day something extraordinary happened. I was in the water talking and listening to Grandfather and my Ancestors when I noticed this presence that I had not noticed before. This presence felt very, very tall. My awareness was that it was a very large entity. I described it as "a massive square stone column with rounded edges similar to stone columns that support huge Cathedral ceilings." It was tall, stately and beautiful. My experience of angels is not gendered, however, I use the personal pronoun based on how I sense them. Angels aren't male or female. They are simply angelic beings.

This being was looming there so majestically. I looked up. I couldn't see the top of this majestic column. I wasn't sure what I was experiencing. I couldn't see a bodily form, a head or a face, or arms. I acknowledged the presence and said, "Hi. Thank you for being here with me today." I always start with gratitude. It is a beautiful way to connect. Then I asked the presence its name. I was feeling a tremendous strength from the being. It felt masculine to me, so

I may occasionally use masculine pronouns when referring to this presence. I was very surprised to experience this great, strong angel as shy. This being would not tell me its name.

When I asked, it said, "Doesn't matter. Doesn't matter."

And I said, "I would like to know more about you. If I know your name, I could do a little research and see if others have met you and written about their encounters with you."

The being replied, "No, doesn't matter, doesn't matter." This being appeared so shy and so humble and yet, so powerful; it "didn't matter, didn't matter…"

I said, "Okay," and let it go.

For a long time, several months, it simply showed up every day. Then one day during the summer of 2015, I saw that this being was holding something. It was holding it right in front of its heart in the center of its chest. Remember that this presence is very tall, so what I am seeing is held quite a distance above my head. I asked the being, "What do you have there?"

For many years, I have been wrestling with this notion of writing a book. My life is full of so many rich and wondrous experiences. For years I have been trying to figure out what to do and how to do it. I was wondering if I was supposed to share these personal stories. I feel that I have taken on an important, significant, weighty and exciting task. I received a lot of encouragement to write from students, friends and family.

I looked up at this being, and it answered my question. "This is your book."

"My book? What do you mean?"

And then he said, "I'm holding your book." I was really puzzled by that.

I said, "You're holding my book?"

And he said, "Yes. It's already written."

"It is?" I was surprised to see the book and to hear that it was already written.

And he said, "Yes. All you need to do now is read it and write it down."

"Really? It's all done? I just have to read it and write it down?"

And he said, "Yes. That's all you have to do."

I thought, "Oh my gosh! How can this be?" I don't understand any of this. All I know is there is this being that I have been suspecting is an angel standing in front of me. He is holding my book at his heart, telling me it is done and that I just have to read it and write it down.

This went on for a few days, and the angel came every morning with Grandfather and the Ancestors and the other angelic beings. Every time this angel shows up, there is my book held right at its heart. The book is closed and the cover looks deep red-brown in color. The Angel is supporting it from the bottom edge holding it upright with the front cover facing out.

I had been trying to figure out what I was supposed to do with all of this. My inner dialogue had been quite chaotic. "What was I supposed to do with all of this? How do you read a book that an angel is holding, I mean I've never gotten lessons on how to read a book that an angel is holding? Gee, what am I supposed to do with this?"

I tried a couple more times. "I really would like to know who you are. Could you please tell me who you are?"

Finally, the angel standing before me, holding my book, shared its name with me. He said quietly, "Ari'El."

I thought, "Wow, now I can go learn a little bit more about you. I want to research the way that you've worked in other people's lives. Maybe that information will give me some insight into what I am called to do next."

When I returned home from the pool, I was eager to do some research around the name "Ari'El" that the angel had shared with me. I went to the Internet and searched for the "meaning of Ari'El" at www.behindthename.com. I couldn't believe my eyes. I felt my heart swell and my breath catch. I wept to learn that the Hebrew name Ari'El means 'Lion of God.' (*Ari* means lion; *El* is one of the names for God) To be certain that this was absolutely correct I went to another site, https://en.wikipedia.org/wiki/Ariel and found the same definition for the Hebrew name, 'Ari'El,' 'Lion of God!' I thought, "How can these be coincidences? How can it be that for a major part of my life I've had a spirit helper who comes to me in the form of a Great Lion and then this bashful, powerful, beautiful angel finally reveals its identity to me: its name is Ari'El, Lion of God! I just don't believe that anything that profound could be a coincidence."

In that moment there was a deep joy that filled me with the knowledge of Ari'El's name and identity. My heart was so full. I have known the Great Lion as my closest Spirit Friend and most powerful Spirit Ally for nearly four decades. He is the only one that I trust with my life.

Now I discover something even more amazing about Ari'El. He chose to come to me in the form of a Lion so that I could embrace his presence. He was willing to let go of his identity in order for me to welcome his presence into my life. This has allowed us to share marvelous adventures together without my being totally intimidated by his angelic identity.

Somehow, as awesome as it was to meet that Great Lion all those years ago, it was a presence that I could relate to because of its physical attributes. What a profound awareness when I realized the lengths to which this Archangel went to connect and communicate with me. I was truly important to him. We are truly important to them. It certainly seems to me that they cherish relationships with us.

With this significant piece of information, we now return to my current conundrum: How does one go about reading a book that an angel is holding?

At the beginning of this chapter, I checked in with Ari'El, asking if I could tell the story of our meeting, relationship and the book that he held and Ari'El consented.

I asked, "Ari'El, you told me to read the book you are holding and then to write it down. I don't know how to do that. How can I read a book that you are holding?"

Ari'El responded instantly, "Go home and get your iphone with the recorder in it. I will tell you the stories and you record it into your iphone. Then listen to each story and write it down."

I left the pool and went directly home. I sat on the couch with my iphone. I alerted Ari'El that I was ready for the download. I had no idea how or even if this would work. One at a time he dictated the stories to me. By the end of the day I had nine stories to transcribe.

I was busy writing the stories as I transcribed his words. I needed to take oral storytelling and present it in formatted, readable sentences with good grammar. The next morning after I had worked on the transcription, I noticed that the book Ari'El was holding was now open. Each day that I saw him, the pages had been flipped so that as I progressed, so did the pages in the book.

One day while writing down one of the stories, I was hit by a bombshell of awareness!

"You arrogant soul!" I said to myself as a strong realization came to me.

"You think you wrote this book that Ari'El has dictated to you. In fact, Ari'El has written it about his encounters with you. Ari'El wants you to do this for him because he needs your humanness to get it done. It is so important for him because he wants others to learn through these stories. These are not just your stories; they are his stories. He wants people to know that he and millions of angels are simply waiting for humans to let them into their lives."

The angels can't barge in without our openness to them or an invitation to them. We have free will and they honor that gift in humanity. These stories are Ari'El's way of sharing with humanity and hoping others will wake up to the wonder and beauty that I have been privileged to experience for so many years."

Now I understood. My book is Ari'El's book. All of these experiences, and many more, we have shared. They are our common experiences. They are powerful. I have co-created this book with Ari'El because he asked me to do this for him and for humanity.

Please ask yourself, "How is it that you happen to be reading this book?" Is it perchance that an Angel of God is knocking at your door? Is it perchance that God has much more wonder and awe waiting for you than you can possibly imagine? Don't sit there wondering. All you need to do is say, "Yes!"….and hold on!

EPILOGUE

When I was first introduced to Aslan, I was unsure and felt a little crazy. Most people don't speak of visions for fear of being seen as unstable. Being a Christian pastor, I was very hesitant to share any of this with my congregation(s) or my peers. I wasn't hearing other pastors reporting such events in their lives.

Several years earlier when attending Adult Summer Conference of the Disciples of Christ, we were privileged to have Dr. Margaret Nutting Ralph as our Bible Study Expert for the Week. At one of our gatherings she asked for a show of hands of how many had experienced a vision and never told any one. I was amazed to see how many hands went up. That moment was full of encouragement. The realization that I might be able to share these stories one day was an overwhelming thought.

Teaching in seminaries and universities, I have shared some of my stories with students. They encourage me emphatically to "WRITE THEM DOWN because others need to hear them." One

Doctoral student begged me to write them. When she saw that I wasn't getting around to doing it, she offered to transcribe them for me from a recording.

Another time I heard that the worst thing one can do is share the name or any information about a Spirit Helper with others because it allows an energetic opening for someone who might want to cause some evil doing. This shook me up a bit; so, I very seldom and only to select people would share these and other stories.

Julie Swanson, Ojibway Medicine Woman and Disciple of Christ Pastor, became my confidant and guided me through this murky terrain. She advised that in my situation it was different. When I questioned her, this was her response: "You are to tell others about your Dreams and Visions. You are to share the name of your Spirit Helper because you are to teach others that they too are capable of such guidance. And," Julie added, "You will be protected."

Here I have shared some of these incredible stories. There are so many more to report.

ABOUT THE AUTHOR

Carol Vaccariello is very real, very grounded, very hard working; she is a keen serious listener and teacher, a seasoned student and administrator. Through her spiritual coaching practice, she shares and teaches the wisdom of her experience. She is committed to service and lives a simple life style of service to others. Her spiritual path is rich and diversified. She has lived and worked as a Catholic sister for five years; as a wife and supporter of a union organizer in Ohio for thirty years; as a Protestant pastor for thirty-one years; as Director of the Doctor of ministry program at the Ecumenical Theological Seminary for five years; as co-director of the Doctor of ministry program at the University of Creation Spirituality for nine years; and later at Wisdom University; she has served as an interim pastor at a number of UCC and DOC churches, often called in to resolve conflicts or to help heal wounded congregations. Culturally, Carol is grounded in the Italian Strega tradition which informs her Earth based, Wise Woman, Healer, Native knowing of our cosmic home. She practices deep ecumenism and is interfaith embracing a Braided Spirituality(braidedway.org). Carol composes sacred music, chants and dances, touching deep awareness and freeing revelatory inspiration. Her feet are very much on the ground. She is an Elder guiding others on their spirit paths. The fruits of her healthy and giving life are there for anyone to see. She is a woman of courageous spiritual evolution.

Printed in the United States
By Bookmasters